CURIOUS
MATRIX

QUESTIONS I ALWAYS WANTED TO ASK

.

Domagoj Pernar

CURIOUS MATRIX: Questions I always wanted to ask

Self-published by Domagoj Pernar

Contact: domagoj@curiousmatrix.com

Website: www.curiousmatrix.com

Book and cover design by Domagoj Pernar

Pictures and illustrations by Domagoj Pernar

ISBN: 978-953-49833-0-0

Zagreb, December 2021

To my late father, Stjepan Pernar!

You taught me the importance of being curious.
You were tougher than the rest.
You were better than the rest.
You were never at rest.
You were my father.
This is for you.

CONTENTS

Intro

There are people who think a lot about the world, ask questions about everything, and generally people who are curious about various topics. On the other hand, there are people who are not interested in anything and just go through life without curiosity. It is much easier for these people because they usually do not care about anything outside their observable universe. I'm not like that. I have always been interested in various topics in the spectrum of life. This spectrum awoke the curiosity in me in a way that I always read various sources of knowledge because, especially nowadays, there really isn't one version of the truth about almost any topic. And so, at one point, I decided it would be worthwhile to put my questions and thoughts on paper. Being aware that I am not a popular or known author, I still decided to write down my own thoughts and create a book out of it. Because, in fact, the minds of many people are curious, and they wonder about a variety of topics, so why not write a book that goes exactly in that direction. You don't have to be an expert on many topics to be able to contemplate them. Our brain creates hundreds of topics every second, and a good portion of people try to calm it down through meditation or similar methods. And that's fine, but topics that interest us individually end up on the surface again, and we have to or want to deal with them in some way. And so, every time something interesting came to my mind, I decided to contemplate it and write it down.

What you are going to read is by no means scientifically accurate in every way or a complete truth, but it is one man's reflections on different topics with a pinch of creativity. A good part of the book is supported by various research, but a good portion is open to the imagination. That's why I wrote this book, to share my view, which can be correct, it can be fictional and imaginable, but it is curious and explorational in many ways. That is the essence of writing - to explore your mind while bringing fiction closer to nonfiction.

The book consists of 18 chapters that are not connected subjectwise but are somehow connected in curiosity. Those chapters are structured to make you question your foundations of thinking and consider difficult subjects. Whether those are; a future world with sex robots, a world without weapons, or perhaps a world without electricity, I think they are very interesting questions that are open to interpretation.

Reading this book is not intended to be linear, so use your curiosity and open the chapters in your own way. In the way your curiosity works.

I have to understand the world, you see.

— RICHARD FEYNMAN

What will sex robots do to humanity?

"Everything in the world is about sex except sex. Sex is about power."
– OSCAR WILDE

Sex robots will become a regular part of society. Unfortunately, it seems inevitable. Primarily this is because we humans are always thinking about ways to invent new things and improve the current life experience. It is in human nature. However, we should sometimes be wise enough to decide that even though we have the ability to do something (or build something), maybe we should choose not to do it. For example, the Manhattan Project was a research and development project happening during World War II that yielded the first nuclear weapons. The United States led it with help from the United Kingdom and Canada. Maybe if the team of scientists and politicians included in that project had enough wisdom to decide not to do it even though they had enough scientific and engineering knowledge, the history of the world would be completely different than it is now. Maybe better, maybe worse; we can't know.

How is this related to Sex Robots, you may think? Well, the invention of Sex Robots could potentially reinvent human society and interactions as we know them. And probably not in a good way. In history, humans' desire to have sex with something inhuman is not new. So, one would think that we are somehow connected with those weird desires only in recent times. Not really. For example, in ancient Greek mythology, Pygmalion fell in love with one of his sculptures that came to life. Essentially, the young sculptor was disgusted by vulgar real women, so he sculptured a virginal maiden for himself. The basic idea of that myth was a popular subject for Victorian-era English playwrights where, for example, George Bernard Shaw had a play with the same name. Although the Pygmalion myth is often presented in modern times as a romantic love story, the tale is an unnerving description of one of the first female android sex partners in Western history.

Fast forward to modern times, and we can see a lot of flirting with the idea of sex robots. In two relatively recent movies, Her and Ex Machina, filmmakers explored an intriguing concept; whether humans will fall in love with AI or robots and want to have sex with them in some way. Both movies have exciting plots and potentially even more exciting consequences. In those movies, the writer explores the idea of love and relationship more than the idea of pure sex and pleasure. And this idea exists nowadays more than ever.

Consequently, the product of imagination to create almost real sex robots is here in our lives. You can buy all kinds of sex dolls created from different materials on the market. Some of them are pure silicon and cannot make any interactions, but some (and especially in recent times) have built-in AI capabilities, and they can interact with real humans. And those interactions can vary, from pure sex and pleasure to somewhat coherent speaking. Of course, the latter is also rather significant, but in my opinion, sex capabilities will be the first to blame for transforming society as we know it.

So, let's create an imaginary person in a not-so-far-away future where sex dolls and robots are affordable and realistic. Let's call that person Adam. One day Adam comes home after his stressful day at work, says "Hi" to his wife, and they carry on in normal couple conversation. Later that night, his wife, Ella, goes to bed, and Adam starts researching sex robots. Soon enough, he finds out that sex robots are not only affordable (1000-5000 dollars), but they are looking great and can be delivered to his doorway in 5 working days. After a couple of beers, Adam decides to order one. What the heck? It can be exciting and potentially spice things up in a relationship, Adam is thinking to himself. On Friday next week, a sex robot named Lucy arrives, and everything starts to change. Ella is not really satisfied with the new product in the house, but she accepts it/her as it is. They even begin to have mutual fun with Lucy. But then, after a couple of days, many things start to fall apart. First, Adam starts to have sex with Lucy on an hourly basis because now he can explore all his sexual desires. Second, he begins to leave his job to have sex with Lucy on every possible occasion. Third, he starts to ignore his wife as the days go by. Fourth, he is now sitting all day long on his couch together with Lucy doing weird things. Fifth, he starts to fall in love with Lucy even though his mind tells him this is not normal. Six, he loses his job. Seven, his wife leaves him. Eight, he is still satisfied with Lucy because he can have sex all day, every day. Nine, he can order additional parts for Lucy, so she looks different every couple of months. Ten, he completely loses connection with real-life and with everything normal and sane.

Now multiply this with a couple of hundred million or even billions of men. How many men would try out Lucy if she was affordable and available? And how many would get addicted? I would say we that can talk about a pretty significant percentage of men. Of course, there will also be male robots, and the percentages of women desiring one will also probably skyrocket. What will happen with human relationships, reproduction, economy, and sanity if all those examples become a reality? In my opinion, things could get really messy in our world in only one generation (or even in 20-30 years). I can easily imagine 10% of men not wanting to do anything but only hang out with their sex robots. Then I can imagine that another 10-20 percent of people will completely lose interest in other (or any) gender. If an additional 10-20% of people decide somehow to introduce sex robots in their lives, then we are talking about 50% of the adult population. That's a considerable number to change the fundaments of any society. Repercussions of only small percentages of people deciding to build any kind of relationship with sex robots are of incredible proportions. There will be fewer children in the world. There will be fewer proper relationships, and those are some of the fundaments of our society. Then some ultra-leftist groups will start to make rallies for sex robots, asking for their special toilettes (even though Lucy and their robot sisters don't need one).

In summary, we are potentially fucked big time in the future with this imaginary scenario, and I mean that literally (by sex robots) and figuratively. Even though this sounds harsh, try to imagine if sex robots become a reality like today's smartphones are. Nobody predicted 30 years ago how much disruption smartphones would make. In that way, nobody can predict what sex robots will do to humanity, but if they impact it only in a small percentage compared to what smartphones did, well, then we are in one hell of a ride which will change the whole fabrics of society. Some day, will there be an international beauty pageant for sex robots? I think it will be, and this is enough to think twice about the development of those "gadgets." The same goes for some categories of virtual reality products, but that's another (but very connected) story.

How would a human child develop without external influence and love?

"Love is meant to nurture and not enslave."
– VICTOR VOTE

Some animals come to this world more self-sufficient than others. Think about many documentaries you watched where an animal is born and then almost instantly starts to walk or swim and is practically capable of solo living. Then think about humans and how helpless human babies are when they are born and how helpless they are for many years to come.

There are many different bonds, connections, and relationships between newborn children of various animals (including humans). For example, the bond between an orangutan mother and her young is one of the strongest we know in nature. Throughout the first two years of their lives, the young rely entirely on their mothers for both food and transportation. The moms stay with their young for five to seven years, teaching them where to find food, what and how to eat, and different techniques for building a sleeping shelter. Furthermore, female orangutans visit their mothers until they reach the age of around 15 years old.

Elephants are also fascinating. They live in a matriarchal society, which means that other females in their group help in raising baby elephants. By watching the adults, the calf learns which plants to eat and how to behave in a certain way. Mother elephants are very careful with their young ones, and they live with them for a rather long period. On the other hand, male elephants mostly live a solitary existence.

Some predators are also there for their young ones for a prolonged time. Namely, cheetah mothers raise their young in isolation. They move their litter every couple of days to prevent a build-up of odor that predators can track. After 16 to 18 months of training as hunters, the young cheetahs can finally leave their mothers. The cubs then form a family group that will stay together for another six months or so.

On the other hand, many animals are not so helpful to their young ones. For example, harp seals, who are cute beyond imagination, well, in fact, they are doing something completely different. Mothers of these gorgeous little ones are highly devoted for the first twelve days. They do not eat at all during that period. However, once the feeding is over, that's it for mother-child bonding — she's immediately out of there, finding a partner and mating again. Unlike many other species with such abrupt detachment from their mother's care, the harp seal child can't go on to survive on its own just yet. Instead, it is left alone on the ice for the next month and a half, leaving it extremely vulnerable to different predators. Typically, babies lose a significant portion of their body weight (on average around half of the body weight) during this starvation period. Then, if they survive for the next couple of weeks, they are ready to swim and start hunting for food. With a "wonderful" childhood like this, it's no surprise that at least 20-30% of all pups die during their first year.

There are other similar examples. Pandas, one of the

cutest living creatures, can do some horrible things (as per our standard). Namely, although pandas often have twins (50% of the time on average), they rarely care for more than one of them. Mom chooses the weaker of the two babies and starts ignoring him or her in favor of the stronger sibling. Interesting approach, huh?

However, we can all agree that human-animal goes into a completely different category than anything else in the animal world. First, we have a very long gestation period. Only elephants and maybe a couple of other animals come even close. The average gestation period of humans is 280 days or 40 weeks, while elephants have a more extended gestation period of around 640 to 660 days or 95 weeks. Additionally, giraffes, rhinos, camels, walruses, whales, dolphins, sharks, tapirs, and donkeys carry their child longer than humans. That's about it. Since there are around 8,7 million species on Earth by some science approximations, one can easily say that we humans are in the top corner when the gestation period is concerned.

Love and carrying are even more pronounced in humans. As mentioned at the beginning of this chapter, some animals are magnificent mothers (and fathers); however, nothing comes even close to human mothers and fathers (well, at least in most cases). In the majority of situations, human children and their parents stay in contact their whole life. Additionally, human children are incapable of living on their own for many years to come. Sometimes this is 16 years, sometimes 18, sometimes 24, but it can also happen that a human child stays in a "parent's nest" for their whole life.

Furthermore, one thing that is quite important in human life is love. Love is rather hard to define. It is different than caring for someone. Love consists of a range of strong and positive emotional and mental states, from the most sublime virtue or a good habit to the deepest interpersonal affection and the simplest pleasure. Ancient Greek philosophers named five different forms of love: familial love, friendly love or platonic love, romantic love, guest love, and divine love. Modern authors have recognized further varieties of love: unreturned (unrequited) love, empty love, companionate love, consummate love, infatuated love, self-love, and polite or courtly love.

Apart from different categories of love, evolutionary psychology tried to provide various reasons for love as a survival tool. As mentioned, humans are dependent on parental help for a large portion of their lifespans compared to other mammals. Love was therefore seen as a mechanism to promote parental support of children for this extended timeframe. Additionally, researchers as early as Charles Darwin himself identified unique features of human love compared to other mammals and credited love as the main factor for creating social support systems that enabled the development and growth of the human species. And this is very important for this chapter because the question revealed at the beginning is: How would a human child develop without external influence and love?

Unfortunately, in somehow modern history, there have been experiments with real children asking the same question with actual consequences. In the United States, in 1944, an experiment was performed on 40 newborn babies to determine whether individuals could prosper alone on basic physiological needs but without affection/love. Twenty newborn babies were placed in a special facility where caregivers would feed them, change their diapers and provide all needed physiological care, but they would not do anything else. The caregivers had been ordered not to look at or touch the babies more than what was necessary. Also, they were instructed not to communicate in the room with babies at all. All their physical needs were attended to rigorously, and the environment was kept sterile, with none of the babies becoming ill.

The experiment was stopped after four months, by which time at least half of the babies had died. At least two more died even after being rescued and brought into a more natural and familial environment. There was no physiological cause for the babies' deaths as they were all physically very healthy. Each baby died in a specific behavioral pattern. Namely, there was a period of time where they stopped verbalizing completely with their caregivers, and mostly they also stopped moving, crying, and changing expressions. After that kind of behavior, death followed shortly.

As this was taking place, in a separate facility, the second group of twenty newborn infants were raised with all their basic physiological needs provided and with the addition of love and warmth from their caregivers. This time, luckily, the outcome was as expected, and no deaths were encountered. The conclusion was that nurturing and love is very important need in humans. Additionally, many researchers discovered that human babies need human touch in their development. Touch can ease pain, lift depression and impact all kinds of psychological challenges. But basic touch is even more important than this as babies who are not held, snuggled, and hugged enough can stop growing, and if the situation lasts long enough, they can even die.

There were also many weird experiments during history, especially if we go back a couple of centuries. To be more precise, in the thirteen century, when the German king, Frederick II, conducted a diabolical experiment intended to determine what language children would naturally grow up to speak if never spoken to. Funny enough (if the word funny can be placed in the same paragraph as this disastrous experiment), he, of course, thought they would naturally speak German. Having these insane thoughts, he took babies from their mothers at birth and moved them to the care of nurses who were prohibited from speaking during that time. But a second rule was also imposed, and this was not to touch the babies. Frederick's experiment was shortened to his great disappointment, but not before something tragically significant regarding human nature was revealed. As you probably guessed, the babies grew up to speak no language at all because they all died.

So basically, what did all those experiments demonstrate to us? Well, it is obvious – people are social beings who need love both in their young days and when they are older. That is a fact. Now, in current times we are increasingly dissocializing, and the human touch is getting worse and worse year by year. Imagine what will happen in 10 or 50 years. If robot nannies bring up our babies, what will human relationships look like? What will the love look like? Those are questions that we all need to ask ourselves and see where we are going with all those technology "advancements" that are perhaps not needed. Don't get me wrong, numerous technological advancements are great for many things in our lives but perhaps not so much for real human connections. Namely, we can all witness that real nurturing and human touch, in many cases, only happens on paper. One must surely agree that parents are spending less and less time with their children in pursuit of "fake" happiness, that is money and extreme careerism. The results of all those behaviors will be seen in the current young generation and especially in generations that are not yet born.

What if people couldn't lie?

"History is a set of lies agreed upon."
– NAPOLEON BONAPARTE

Lying is specific virtue that only humans and perhaps some other apes have. I am using the word 'perhaps' here because it is not crystal clear if some apes also have the ability to produce lies or deceive their fellow apes in order to get what they want. Indeed, scientists studied the behaviors of apes for a longer period of time and noticed that they could develop the ability to lie and deceive in order to get food or to mate. The team analyzed behavioural patterns of 24 different primate species and found deceptive behaviour is more common in species that co-operate more. That's interesting and very much connected to us – homo sapiens – as we are cooperative by nature. Based on that, scientists hypothesized that our ultimate ability to lie to each other probably evolved because of our cooperative nature.

There are more very interesting anecdotal examples in the animal kingdom. It has been found that male chimpanzees are especially virtuous in lying and deceiving in order to get away with sex that is forbidden by the socially powerful. As we know, there is a hierarchy structure in the ape world, and the alpha male gets the most sexual activity, and he can choose partners as he wishes. Similar to the human world, isn't it? However, it seems like females also have comparable capabilities. In his book Chimpanzee Politics: Power and Sex among Apes, primatologist Frans De Waal writes about an adolescent female ape (called Orr) at Arnhem Zoo who would scream during intercourse. However, she didn't only have sex with the alpha male but also with younger males. Since she was screaming, the alpha male heard that and almost always interrupted them. Eventually, after several interruptions, Orr learned to suppress her screams when copulating with lower-ranking males, but she still continued her screams while having sex with the alpha. This again sounds awfully similar to human life and behavioural patterns related to sexual intercourse and relationships.

On the other hand, competition also plays a big role in the desire to deceive someone as it seems. Namely, Frans wanted to observe if chimpanzees will try to deceive one another during a simple experiment. So, he used a box of grapefruits to demonstrate the point that perhaps chimpanzees will try to deceive one another. While they were locked in their sleeping rooms, he brought the box out to the public area and buried the grapefruit in the sand. He only left a small portion of grapefruit still uncovered. He wanted to test chimpanzees' behaviour and potential deception if one of them in the group noticed that buried grapefruit and others didn't. The other day Frans and other researchers placed the empty box in the public area, and as expected, all chimpanzees rushed for their fruits, as they are used to finding fruits in those kinds of boxes. This time, unfortunately, they didn't find anything. However, one young male, as it seems, did notice buried fruit, but he didn't want to "tell" anyone else by digging the fruits so everyone could see. He instead slowly dug up the fruits and ate them peacefully when no one was looking. That's deceiving 101.

And so, I digress too much about monkeys; however, I

think it is an important prelude to understanding why humans lie so that we could potentially imagine what would happen if we suddenly lost that ability. As we learned, chimpanzees often deceive each other and their human caretakers; that much is clear, but we don't know if they are aware that it is morally wrong as we are when we're deceiving someone.

We humans – we are aware. Well, for the most part. That is if we exclude humans with a mental disorder in which the person habitually or compulsively lies. Yes, that is a thing, and it is called mythomania or pathological lying. Nevertheless, a big majority of people do not have that disorder, yet we lie all the time. According to a study conducted by University of Massachusetts's psychologist Robert S. Feldman and published in the Journal of Basic and Applied Social Psychology, most people lie in everyday conversation when they are trying to seem likable and knowledgeable. The study, published in the journal's June issue, found that sixty percent of people lied at least once during a short (5-15 minute) conversation and told an average of two to three lies. The study additionally found that lies told by men and women differ in content, though not much in quantity. Feldman mentioned how the results indicated that men do not lie more than women or vice versa, but that men and women actually lie in different ways and because of different triggers. "Women were more likely to lie to make the person they were talking to feel good, while men lied most often to make themselves look better," Feldman stated.

Additional studies suggest that 'like strategists,' we gauge the field and calculate if saying something will be of benefit before making a decision. In one well-known experiment, conducted in the mid-1980s by developmental psychologist Michael Lewis, children were asked to NOT peek at a toy that was left alone in a room with them. They were then examined about whether their curiosity had led to action. While most kids did look at the toy, a large number of children continued to lie about it. A similar experiment was conducted with children and cakes. They lied again about their actions. That clearly shows that we're born with the ability to lie. Now, while most lies are harmless and we sometimes tell them almost unconsciously, there are also lies people are making that have an impact on a grand scale. BIG LIE is an actual term defined as a propaganda technique used for political purposes. The expression (German: große Lüge) was created by Adolf Hitler, when he dictated his 1925 book Mein Kampf (which by the way means My Struggle), about the use of a lie so "colossal" that no one would believe that someone "could have the impudence to distort the truth so infamously." Hitler also believed the technique of lying was used by Jews to blame Germany in World War I. In Mein Kampf, he "famously" stated:

"If you tell a big enough lie and tell it frequently enough, it will be believed."

"The great masses of the people will more easily fall victims to a great lie than to a small one."

Now, Hitler is not the only one who used big lies for enormous criminal purposes that affected humanity greatly in a negative way. There are thousands of examples of individuals but also groups of people or organizations. For example, the big economic crisis of 2008 probably wouldn't happen if big bankers didn't lie bluntly to citizens. Actually, almost all big crises in the world happened because people, organizations, or whole nations lied to other people, organizations, or nations. Lies are perhaps the biggest contributor to all evil in the world, yet humans probably wouldn't develop as they did without this ability. Historian and author Yuval Noah Harari extensively describes this in his book

Sapiens: A Brief History of Humankind. He explained how Homo sapiens' ability to create myths and fictions (and lies) is the very thing that has enabled us to create communities. And without communities, we wouldn't become what we are today – the most successful species on the Earth (for now). Just imagine if we were all alone by ourselves, without communities. We wouldn't build or invent much. And what keeps us in communities is a belief system that is based on fiction, a.k.a. lie. I wouldn't want to offend anyone with the following statement as I respect all religions and beliefs, but we can all probably agree that religious stories are pure fiction; nevertheless, without belief in those stories or their end goal, it would be hard to keep people together. This is, of course, only one example but nevertheless an example on a big scale. A smaller example would be when you tell your first girlfriend or boyfriend that you will be together forever. That is clearly a lie (in most cases), but for sure, that lie keeps you together.

So obviously, lies are both good and bad for society, but it seems we couldn't live without them. Or could we? Let's examine an imaginary society where the whole population simply cannot lie. They don't even know what the word lie means. The world without lies would be vastly different from the one we know - that much is understood. Starting from examples of criminal deeds both on individual and community levels. Would those deeds still happen? Yes, for sure but on a much lower level. Namely, currently, more than 400,000 homicides worldwide happen each year. Globally less than 1% of deaths are from homicide, but in some countries, it is as high as 10%. Without the ability to lie, those numbers would go down greatly. Because when someone kills somebody, the killer is hoping he or she will get away with it by not telling the truth. If the killer doesn't have the ability to lie, he would probably tell someone immediately that he committed homicide. This would lead to arrest and whole life in prison. Not a great situation to be, is it? Some people would still commit homicide but mostly when they are completely out of their minds.

But what about lies and human relationships as such? By that, I mean close friends, family, and love relationships. Well, those relationships wouldn't function as they do today. Not even close. People are telling lies constantly, some bigger and some really small ones. As mentioned previously, the University of Massachusetts study found that 60% of people can't go ten minutes without lying. Nevertheless, telling lies is an important part and, in many cases, a benign part of each relationship. Knowing that, it can be easily understood that many relationships couldn't work without lies. Some bigger lies, like adultery, would destroy many love relationships immediately. Because imaginary John would come home after having sex with his imaginary friend Julia and immediately tell his wife Susan what happened today. And probably every possible detail because Susan would be furious and curious. So, Susan and John would probably break up soon after. Ok, adultery may be a big deal, but couples would also fight about many smaller things if they couldn't lie. John would wake up one day and say to Susan that she is fat or vice versa. Anyhow, there could be thousands of such examples. So, lies would for sure negatively impact some love relationships.

The same goes for friendships. Well, at least for the majority of friendships. Everybody is aware of saying: 'You can tell everything to your true friends." While this quote is nice to say in a sentence to your friend after a couple of beers, it is not true, as, in the overwhelming majority of friendships, there are still lies. So, without lies, there would be a great disturbance among friends around the world. One could conclude that without lies, relationships would not exist at all. Or at least not in this shape or form as we know them today.

I am assuming all this based on parameters of current society and homo sapiens, which did develop with the ability to lie and then taking the hypothesis of removing that ability. However, we became what we are through hundreds of thousands of years of evolution. An evolution that included the ability to lie. So, how would we develop if we hadn't had the ability to lie from the beginning? Well, in that case, I think relationships, and everything else for that matter, would function completely different than what I described in previous pages. If people evolved without lies and still don't have that capability, then perhaps they would be good and sincere in their pure essence. Then maybe there wouldn't be any nasty and mean activities in any relationship because people would have known that they couldn't get away with it in the first place. It is interesting to hypothesize if homo sapiens would even exist today without lies. Maybe we would self-destruct as a species. Maybe we would miss all the development and still be in the stone age. I mean, many developments through human history can be attributed to our capability to lie or, even more so, our ability to imagine something which is not true. Those dreamers who have great ideas and inventions, in most cases, cannot come through if they can't lie, even just a little bit. How would someone sell the idea of electricity, cars, planes, or mobile phones without at least a small amount of lie at the beginning of the idea? Products and inventions need investment, belief, and trust from other people to see the daylight, and almost always, the inventor or seller needs to evangelize their potential product in a way to represent (something) as being larger, better, or more efficient than it really is. This is, by definition, an exaggeration or some form of lie. People couldn't exaggerate if they didn't have the capability to lie.

Therefore, one can conclude that capability of lying is the main factor in human development; hence, without lying, we would still probably be an average animal with standard (and natural) desires and needs. Perhaps without lies, we would still live like early homo sapiens 100 000 years ago. We will never know this, but potentially we'll see the world without lies in the near future with the invention of different brain scanners and chips implanted in our heads. Scientists are working on that in one way or another. It wouldn't be impossible to have humans walking on Earth in, say, 2050, who could read the mind of other humans, thus basically nullifying the lying ability of the human race. Whenever and however this technology develops, it has to be introduced to humans slowly and gradually since it diminishes one of the main postulates of our evolution and our current society – our ability to lie and deceive.

Is social media leading society into oblivion & abyss?

"Tolerance will reach such a level that intelligent people will be banned from thinking so as not to offend the imbeciles."
– FYODOR MIKHAILOVICH DOSTOEVSKY

Many people in the world, and especially experts in the field, agree that social media is somehow dangerous to society. Yes, the main slogans and catchwords of those exact social media companies are: "We are connecting the world," "We're taking you closer to your loved ones," "We're demigods of your social status." Ok to be fair, the latter one perhaps not so much, but you get the picture.

In reality, social media influenced people and society in such a profound way that this 'connection' in the virtual world is, in most cases, pure illusion. And this illusion is impacting every element of society as we know it.

For example, Chamath Palihapitiya, who joined Facebook in 2007 and became its vice president for user growth, said he feels "tremendous guilt" about the company he helped make. At Stanford's talk, he told the audience: *"I think we have created tools that are ripping apart the social fabric of how society works."* Now, those are very important words coming from someone deeply in the industry. And he is not the only one. Sean Parker, ex-Facebook president, co-founder of Napster, Plaxo, Causes, and investor in many other companies, criticized Facebook at an Axios event, saying, *"God only knows what it's doing to our children's brains."* He also expressed concerns about the role of Facebook in society, saying that it exploits a vulnerability in human psychology as it creates a *"social-validation feedback loop."* Those are just a few examples as many other people, in and outside of the industry, state similar things about Facebook, Instagram, Tik Tok, or any other social media sites and services. If people in the industry are concerned about those social networks or, to be more precise – what those social networks do to our society, then I think it would be reasonable that every person on Earth should be concerned at least a little bit. With that, let's dive a bit deeper and try to categorize exactly which aspects of society are most vulnerable because of social media and what could develop out of it if we continue going in the same direction and with the same or even accelerated pace.

So, let's start with the impact on individual people with additional emphasis on younger members of this society. According to a ScienceDaily article published in 2019, mental health issues increased significantly in young adults over the last decade. To put this into perspective, there is no corresponding increase in older adults, according to research published by the American Psychological Association. Now, this is rather interesting, but probably many of us already expected similar results. Why? Well, because in the last decade, two very important ingredients have become a standard part of our day-to-day lives, and those are smartphones and social media. Even though social media, and for sure smartphones, are used by older adults, average daily usage is not even comparable. And thus, we see such a big impact on younger people and a much smaller impact on people who are currently in their 50's, 60's and 70's. Actually, I would say, the older you are, the least negative impact of social networks you have. This is easily understandable, but let's see the reasons why depression, anxiety, and other mental health issues are on the rise with the younger population.

Primarily, due to the overuse of social networks, people over time begin to act differently in order to fit into some popular behavioral models. We can look at it as a small virtual world in which each individual is his own actor and his own hero. Everyone wants to show themselves to the world in the best way but only while the stage lights, aka social networks, are turned on. When the stage lights go out, then many return to their not-so-interesting and glamorous lives. Such a model of behavior or such actions literally leads to a change in the personality of people, especially young people, because they maintain a concept of constant comparison with others. And therefore, if you are not popular in that world compared to some imaginary celebrity or virtual friend, then you become more and more depressed and anxious every day. There are thousands of examples of teenagers around the world who have started starving just because someone on social media told them they look slightly fat. It is amazing how much impact this has since a young person is put literally to condemnation and comparison to the whole world. And voluntarily! It certainly cannot end well and cannot have good consequences for one's own mind and self-seeing. In addition, constant monitoring of other lives and events leads to information overload, which then again leads to depression and anxiety.

This is really the first time in history that we have such a social construct in which all people participate on some public stage, voluntarily share pictures with the whole world and argue with a stranger from another continent about whose dress or hairstyle is better. Pretty amazing! Add to that the fact that most people are by nature not adapted to the "world stage" that is a social media platform. The average fool today has more followers or greater reach than Aristotle, Seneca, Marcus Aurelius, or any other historic thinker or statesmen once had. And what he or she or they do with that reach - they mostly share pictures of ass, tits, or stupid memes. And it is precisely this incredible amount of nonsense consumed every day by billions of people that in turn contributes to general confusion and mental problems.

So, I named only several examples and scenarios on how social networks are contributing negatively to the mental state of society. There are many others, and books can be written on this topic alone, but let's explore additional scenarios of how social networks are impacting society in a negative way or how they will impact it in an imaginary but rather possible scenario in the near future.

This scenario is related to jobs and the sustainability of the economy in the world of social networks. Without going deep into macro and microeconomics, I think we can all agree that the sustainability of this economic model depends very much on jobs. That is, to be more precise, that most people are expected to work until retirement so that the flow of money is constantly circulating and so that the older generations receive a pension based on the solidarity model. That model is not the best, as I contemplate in the chapter related to retirement, but it is a system that (for now) works. And it works because people choose careers that in one way or another contribute to the economy and enable them to work until so-called retirement. However, nowadays, more and more people do not want to do "ordinary" jobs and decide to pursue a career as a "star of social networks." And that's great, everyone has the right to choose whatever they want, but it seems to me that a lot of people don't think about the sustainability of their career choices in the longer run. Namely, if a person is 20 years old and has a hundred thousand followers on Instagram and earns some solid money, that is perfectly fine. However, if we go a little deeper into the topic, then we see that it is (for the most part) largely unsustainable for a longer period. That is, a lot of so-called social network stars & influencers are popular only for the sake of beauty, youth, or, for example, showing their buttocks from all angles. And that's okay. But let's try to imagine that same kind of career 10 or 20 years into the future. Will they continue to photograph his or her ass in all poses advertising thongs, or will they reshape their career into something else? If so, in what exactly? Suddenly, while youth passes and beauty is no longer a factor that enables the sale of some goods or advertisements, eh then we come to potential problems. And ok, someone can put up a counterargument saying that such changes in the work environment and career choices have always been in society and always will be, but this time I think it's about something completely different.

All the time during history, people were also saying that the economy would collapse, and that people would lose their jobs because of some new technology. Just think of the industrial revolution or the invention of computers - many have said that millions will lose their jobs. And many did, but also many started doing some other jobs. However, what is different today is that most social media influencers don't know how to do anything else, and more importantly, they don't want to do anything else. And so, are we going to watch those same people ("influencers") in their 50s or older showing themselves in thongs on Instagram or Tik Tok? I don't think we will. I think there will be some radical economic changes much sooner. Just imagine all those millions of young people who will inevitably grow old and social networks will overwhelm them in one way or another. How will they make a living in that case? Most very difficult, I would say. Some will figure it out quickly enough and reshape their careers, but many won't, and then they'll end up on some kind of state aid. And if that happens to enough people, then the system will surely fall to its knees.

If I, as a layman, think about this particular topic, then surely world economists, strategists, and leaders think about it as well. Certainly, people in the World Economic Forum in Davos are discussing the direction of the young generation and what we can expect from them in 20 or 30 years. It's a very important topic and looking at today's teens who are interested in absolutely nothing but Tik Tok or similar things, it certainly becomes a topic of concern. We can't all be social media influencers, and it seems that most young people want just that.

According to a recent survey, about 86% of young Americans stated that they would like to be influencers. Well, Houston, we have a problem. A lot of these young people will be left disappointed and at the same time unprepared for the many other jobs on the market.

As I previously mentioned, social networks paint a fake picture of a world where everyone compares themselves to everyone else, and everyone would like to be little stars in their virtual world. Such a model distorts reality which then fuels desires and dreams in young people that are not realistic. This unreality further encourages the creation of an economic tower of cards that could collapse very quickly. Let's hope it doesn't go in that direction, but looking at many characteristics of today's economy, job choices, and vanity trends, it seems that society has turned into the wrong dead-end street.

With social networks, this dead-end street is not lonely as there are many other reasons why social media could lead society to the abyss. I already mentioned the potential for depression, anxiety, and hypothesis about economic problems. Going further, probably everyone could agree how social networks are destroying what we once knew as friendly human relationships. Of course, those are still here, especially among older people, but bit by bit, social media is changing aspects of human behavior and especially human relationships with other humans. Basically, in one sentence, we could say that relationship between humans and mobile phones is getting stronger while the relationship between humans and other humans is getting worse.

Taking this into account, it is necessary to consider in which direction society is moving if social networks already have such an impact. In my high school, no one had a mobile device (and I'm 37), and social networks didn't even exist. Despite that or precisely because of that, we tried to meet new people. It was part of a social paradigm. If I wanted to talk to my crush, then I really had to reach out to her and say something. It has always been difficult for everyone. But it was necessary, and I think it was good. Nowadays, it's enough to swipe right in the Tinder app to get a potential sexual partner. And all that is fine, but if we look at a longer period of time in the future, then it doesn't really seem so positive. Namely, human beings have been accustomed to communicating face to face for hundreds of thousands of years. And now, through social networks, we have reduced that form of relationship to the push of a button. So, we threw something out to get something else. But if we throw something out, then that flaw will appear somewhere as a negative thing. And it's just nowadays appearing. More and more, especially young people, are developing various forms of addiction to their devices and social networks while neglecting real human relationships. It is amazing that today we have an extremely large number of people who have millions of followers, and many of those people do not have the courage to go out of their apartment for weeks, and even if they go out, then they are afraid to look anyone in the eyes. That is really a problem if we look far enough into the future. Will this "progress" reach such a level that we will all sit in our apartments constantly and socialize only virtually? Looking at what is happening today, it seems that it is almost inevitable. And does that contributes to the overall progress of the human race, or will we be brought to a similar situation as described in the movie Idiocracy? I would say that, as a society, we recently lean more towards the idiocracy scenario than towards something we can view as progress.

So, to answer the question from the beginning of this chapter – are social networks pushing society to the abyss? I would say yes, little by little, but we'll get there one way or another. Zuck will then have a virtual live meeting with the whole world, saying: "In retrospect, it was inevitable."

World without weapons?

"I know not with what weapons World War III will be fought, but World War IV will be fought with sticks and stones."
– ALBERT EINSTEIN

I see myself as a pacifist by nature and perceive the world with humanitarian and altruistic ideology. I'd like to think that people are very empathic, and nations can function without devastating wars, torture, and abhor. This thinking is, of course, unrealistic, as history exhibits. Nations are almost constantly at war with other nations or internally among themselves. According to historians and researchers Will and Ariel Durant, in their

Lessons of History, there have been approximately 268 scattered years without a war over the past 3,421 years. That's not many, considering the timespan.

John Keegan, who is considered a pre-eminent military historian of this era and the author of more than 20 books, argues that wars started along with the uprise of civilization. In his books "War and Our World" and "A History of Warfare," he discusses different topics from conflicts in early civilizations to modern wars in the previous millennium. With first civilizations and with more advanced knowledge on how to get food and other resources, people and communities created a surplus. Nomad people, of course, found surplus as desirable, so they wanted to steal it somehow, therefore creating conflicts between communities and groups of people. Before that, before civilization and first towns – people didn't have wars. This is not to say that early people didn't have violence. They sure did; their whole life was of somehow violent nature. They needed to be like that to survive. But there weren't "organized" wars *per se*. If John Keegan is correct, then people (Homo sapiens) lived for 180,000 years without wars. Based on that, we could conclude that war is mainly found in only 5 to 10% of our history. So obviously, very early history was without wars, and modern history is filled with devastating wars.

But what about today? What if we just stop producing weapons and abolish them completely? I am completely aware that it is a romantic idea but let's indulge it.

Without weapons and especially powerful weapons such as automatic rifles, armored fighting vehicles, and bombs, wars would surely become relics of history, one could claim. Unfortunately, it is not that simple. Some people argue that powerful atomic and hydrogen bombs are the main reason why we currently don't lead mass world wars such as World War I and World War II. The argument proceeds with elaborating how those weapons are so powerful that no nation can gain anything positive since, with the push of a button, nations who have atomic bombs could destroy the world. Previously nations could rage in the war for years and years since they 'only' had weapons such as small guns or bow and arrows. No nation was in such power that they could destroy another nation in a matter of seconds. Now, if there is a big war happening, the USA could, for example, threaten to initiate their most powerful nuclear weapon, a bomb called B83. Or perhaps Russians still keep their monster bomb somewhere – the Tsar Bomba with code name Ivan. This was the most powerful nuclear weapon ever created and tested. Tsar Bomba unleashed unimaginable energy – now widely agreed to be in the order of 57 megatons, or 57 million tons of TNT. That is more than 1,500 times that of the Hiroshima and Nagasaki bombs combined and ten times more powerful than all the weapons expended during World War II.

Think about that for a second (or a minute). Just what on earth is happening with the human consciousness that people even think about creating such a monster. And then they don't stop on the thought – but they decide to dedicate numerous scientists and efforts to build it and then test it on Earth. Yes, the monster was tested. I mean, thrown in an uninhabited area. And they (USA, Russia) aren't the only ones. Now we have many nations on Earth producing nuclear weapons. As far as we know, nine countries currently have nuclear weapons: the US, UK, Russia, France, China, India, Pakistan, Israel, and North Korea. If those nations decided to go to nuclear war, it would be game over for the planet.

It's hard to fathom that Earth formed over 4.5 billion years ago, and human apes have a real chance of destroying it with their weapons and war games. Oppenheimer was the wartime chief of the Los Alamos Laboratory and is among those who are acknowledged as being the "father of the atomic bomb." The first atomic bomb was detonated on July 16, 1945, in the Trinity test in New Mexico. Oppenheimer later stated that it brought to mind words from the Bhagavad Gita: *"Now I am become Death, the destroyer of worlds."* This quote could be taken literally or figuratively, but people behind nuclear weapons really are or could be destroyers of the world. At that time and also today, the scientific community is divided with their opinions on nuclear weapons and their development. Some are big proponents, and some are big critics from the beginning. Ivan Supek, a Croatian physicist and philosopher, belongs to the latter. Supek was an advocate of total and unconditional nuclear disarmament as he warned about the danger of misuse of atomic energy already in 1944 (fourteen months before the bombing of Hiroshima). He was also one of the founders of the international organization World without the Bomb.

Today we have many such organizations:

- Global Zero, international non-partisan group of 300 world leaders dedicated to achieving the elimination of nuclear weapons.

- Global Initiative to Combat Nuclear Terrorism, international partnership of 83 nations.

- International Campaign to Abolish Nuclear Weapons.

- Parliamentarians for Nuclear Non-Proliferation and Disarmament, global network of over 700 parliamentarians from more than 75 countries working to prevent nuclear proliferation.

- Sōka Gakkai, a peace-orientated Buddhist organization, which held anti-nuclear exhibitions in Japanese cities during the late 1970s and gathered 10 million signatures on petitions calling for the abolition of nuclear weapons.

- Pax Christi International, a Catholic group that took a "sharply anti-nuclear stand."

There are dozens and probably hundreds of others. While this is great, we still have thousands of warheads in the world capable of destroying everything on Earth. In 1986 world was at its peak with the number of nuclear weapons. Around 70,000 nuclear weapons existed at that time. In 2019 there were approximately 3700 active nuclear warheads and around 14000 total nuclear warheads. Many of the decommissioned weapons were simply stored or partially disassembled, but not destroyed.

Based on available data, you could conclude that there is simply too much influence and profit to be gained in the world from producing so many weapons. And you would be right. According to the data released by the Stockholm International Peace Research Institute (SIPRI), it is estimated that arms sales by the world's 25 largest arms-producing and military services companies (arms companies) totalled US$361 billion in 2019. This is huge. To give you perspective, this is similar to the GDP of Norway or around six times the GPD of Croatia. So obviously, there is a lot of interest to continue producing arms and weapons. Not only that it is a huge profit in peacetime, but it is also an even bigger profit when there is a big war happening anywhere in the world. Perhaps this is one of the reasons why we still have perpetual wars in the world.

- Nah, I am just thinking out loud here. It couldn't be.

Consequently, if we would like to see the world without weapons, someone would need to do extensive lobbying with companies producing weapons. That is not an easy task as a good percentage of money from weapon-producing companies goes to political parties and candidates. Some transfers of money, in that case, are transparent while a lot is not. Ergo, octopus' arms in this game of war go very, very deep and wide. But let's imagine all of those 'arms are cut off, and we wake up in a world without any producers of weapons, and all old weapons are destroyed. Romantic world, isn't it? Perhaps at first look.

Probably the USA government would make the biggest move because they have so many troops all over the world. Why would those troops stay in 'enemy' territory if there were no weapons anymore? Would they still *"maintain the peace"* in those territories by using their MMA skills? No, I don't think so. Currently, there are more than one million active US soldiers, comprised of 476,000 regular troops, a 343,000-strong National Guard, and US Army Reserves with 199,000 soldiers. So, all of those people would need to be taken care of somehow. And this is only in the US. China is even bigger. They have 2.18 million active soldiers. And what about the number of soldiers on earth? Well, worldwide, 30,277,850 million people are serving in the armed forces, not including paramilitary units. The total number of armed forces personnel, including reserve military and paramilitary units, is 75,543,487. This is significantly bigger than the whole population of Italy (60,3 million) and just slightly smaller than the population of Germany (83 million).

So here we are only talking about people directly tied with the military in some way or another. There are so many other people and businesses who are doing some contract work for the military, whether it is food catering, schools, or producers of military clothing, just to name a few. And then, there are families of military personnel who, in many cases, depend on money from the military. So, taking all of those into consideration, we could try a ballpark calculation and guess that there are probably hundreds of millions of people somehow dependent on the military. Is it 200 million, is it half a billion? Nobody knows exactly, but it is a significant percentage of the world population. What to do with all those people if we stop producing weapons? I mean, without weapons, the military in its principle does not make any sense, now do they? Of course, the military is very helpful whenever there is some crisis or unpredicted horrific event in the country, but that is not their main purpose. The main purpose is to keep their countries safe and, in some cases, invade other countries. With weapons, of course, not with kung fu movements.

So now, in this imaginary scenario, we have a problem with millions upon millions of unemployed people, and many companies tied to the military are out of business. Not a good first step, one could conclude.

But let's what else might happen, especially having in mind current wars and conflicts between countries and political leaders. Currently, in the world, there are many armed conflicts and 'smaller' wars happening, but they are not so interesting to mass media, so people are mostly not informed. Afghanistan conflict is basically ongoing from 1978 starting with Afghan Civil Wars, continuing to War on 'terror' and today (2021) Taliban – ISIL conflict is still happening with 1007 fatalities already in 2021 at the time of writing this page (January 2021). The Yemeni Crisis is also still ongoing. Then we have the Nagorno-Karabakh conflict, Iraq conflict, Boko Haram insurgency, Tigray War, Syrian Civil War, Libyan conflict, and so on and so on.

So, if we had a magic wand and suddenly all world weapons disappeared, basically all those wars and conflicts would also disappear. At least on paper. People would, of course, build new weapons but for the purpose of this hypothesis, let's imagine this isn't possible. Consequently, in this case, soldiers and warriors are left with nothing but throwing stones at each other, and this is a road with no end, so probably all conflicting parties would withdraw slowly. So far, so good. Retreating from wars and conflicts is for sure a positive thing, at least in most situations.

Moving forward to one very important segment of our society, which for sure couldn't function normally without weapons – the police. As we all know, the police are a constituted body of persons empowered by a state, with the aim to enforce the law, to ensure the safety, health, and possessions of citizens, and to prevent crime and civil disorder. In recent times they are also focused on arresting and beating people who do not wear masks, but that's another story. Their lawful powers include arrest and the use of force legitimized by the state via the monopoly on violence. To enforce rules and control violence majority of police officers carry weapons. In many jurisdictions, those weapons are primarily handguns. There are some exceptions, such as Norway, where police officers carry firearms in their vehicles but not on their duty bells. But overall, in most of the world, weapons are vital for functioning police as we know it today.

Consequently, without weapons, the whole police force would undergo significant change. Perhaps more police officers would be needed. Perhaps they would need to learn different martial art techniques so they could restrain ordinary citizens since they don't have weapons anymore. On the positive side, possibly there would be fewer deaths caused by cops, but on the other hand, we would probably see more violence on the streets. Average burglars and criminals would not be so afraid on the streets; therefore, violence would for sure grow. This is not good, so I would score this segment as a negative impact from "the world without weapons initiative."

And what about normal people and their day-to-day life? Would their lives change significantly if there were no weapons? That's a challenging thing to hypothesize since, in many countries, standard folks do not carry any weapon. I mean, they have knives and all that but mostly not ranged weapons designed for shooting. In 2018, Small Arms Survey reported that there are over one billion small arms distributed globally, of which 857 million (about 85 percent) are in civilian hands. The Small Arms Survey also stated that U.S. civilians alone account for 393 million (about 46 percent) of the total worldwide civilian-held firearms. This is to be expected as the United States has generally relaxed measures on who can own a gun.

The Second Amendment of the United States

Constitution states: "A well-regulated Militia, being necessary to the security of a free State, the right of the people to keep and bear Arms, shall not be infringed." This is not the case in many countries; hence such a big percentage comes from the United States. So, for sure, banning weapons would produce significant resistance in the United States and probably not so much in the majority of other countries. I would say that majority of people wouldn't be significantly impacted by banning weapons. Potentially majority of people would even benefit from it because criminals couldn't rob banks so easily or threaten other people.

A world without weapons is for sure not easy to imagine. If all weapons suddenly disappear today, then the governments would have to think about another way to maintain order. Perhaps they would go back to the more primitive way where normal citizens could be involved in catching criminals. Military power world as we know it still relies more on population and weapon strength rather than technology. That said, perhaps one day, we will not use weapons at all. If AI technologies, surveillance systems, and social credit scoring go live into production worldwide - maybe that will become a turning point in the world without weapons. Is that a good thing or complete doom for humanity, time will tell! Most likely, the latter. But certainly, the best thing that could perhaps diminish weapons and wars for good is people becoming wiser about what life's purpose on Earth really is. As the quote from Harry S. Truman goes, "All will concede that in order to have good neighbors, we must also be good neighbors. That applies in every field of human endeavor." If we could just be good to each other as a person to person and country to country, then we would not need any weapons. But unfortunately, that's a far-fetched utopia.

Impact of too much information on humans, their depression, and anxiety?

"We live in a world where there is more and more information and less and less meaning."
– JEAN BAUDRILLARD

Did you know that depression and anxiety are growing substantially year over year, almost all over the world? There are many reasons ranging from lack of physical activity, lack of security, lack of proper food, and lack of freedom in some cases. On the other hand, one thing that we humans are not lacking is the amount of information we receive every day, hour, and minute. This category is for sure off the charts. And this is also one of the main reasons why so many people are so depressed and suffering from anxiety disorders.

Anxiety and depression almost always go hand in hand, one along with the other. And while anxiety was somehow widely popular during the 1950s and 1960s, depression was not so pronounced. Today we still have a boom of anxiety all over, but now depression is also gaining popularity rather fast. In the recent history of psychiatric diagnosis, this is a rather intriguing question – how come did depression grow so much in recent years, and why is that happening? A possible cause of that could be too much information that we are getting every day. Combine that with the type of information most people are receiving, and we have a big concern on our hands. Most information is focused on our fear emotions. While fear is normal and a good instinct, it should be natural emotion and a survival mechanism and not based on everyday information we receive via mainstream news. When we confront an apparent threat, our bodies respond in specific ways. Physical reactions to fear include sweating, increased heart rate, and high adrenaline levels that make us particularly alert. THIS should not happen constantly. And unfortunately, because of how information is served to us every day, many people trigger their fear mechanisms all day, every day. Adding to this, we know that fear is one of the best mechanisms to control people. Over time this then triggers depression and anxiety while we never realize that the stressor, in this case, is an overflow of negative and unnecessary information.

Information overload dates back to Gutenberg. He basically introduced printing to Europe with his inventions, most notably – the movable-type printing press. This led to a proliferation of printed material that quickly exceeded what a single human mind could absorb in a lifetime. After that, we had many similar inventions that only speeded up the production and replication of a huge amount of information on paper. Photocopier first comes to mind here. And then came the digital world, where everyone could produce and replicate an unimaginable amount of information. With digitization, the internet, and television - information started popping up every second from everywhere. While there are many valuable sources of information, and we should be grateful that we have all world's knowledge literally on our smartphones, relevant and valuable information is hard to find. This is because media companies depend on profit, and they serve us information that is bombastic, thus receiving more clicks which gives them in return more money.

But that kind of bombastic information, which is needless to say mostly negative, is impacting our brains. Many (ex) executives from Facebook, Google, and many others have criticized what is happening today with information overload, and our need for instant dopamine hit, that is – constant new information articles, new notifications, or new likes. Many studies have associated information overload with anxiety and depression, and the trend is getting worse every year. So, it's a lot of stuff we are receiving and processing on a daily basis, but what precisely is the problem? In the article written in Harward Business Review, "Death by Information Overload," Paul Hemp explains it very well:

"Researchers say that the stress of not being able to process information as fast as it arrives - combined with the personal and social expectation that, say, you will answer every e-mail message - can deplete and demoralize you. Edward Hallowell, a psychiatrist and expert on attention-deficit disorders, argues that the modern workplace induces what he calls "attention deficit trait," with characteristics similar to those of the genetically based disorder. Author Linda Stone, who

coined the term "continuous partial attention" to describe the mental state of today's knowledge workers, says she's now noticing "e-mail apnea": the unconscious suspension of regular and steady breathing when people tackle their e-mail. "

Now we are getting to the real problem and impact of information overload. People are even unconsciously changing their behaviors based on the information they receive. So, our behavior is changed, our view of the world is changed, and all that because of media companies making more profit. This is for sure alarming if you're looking at it with an awakened brain. How much can our baseline be changed based on the type of information we're served every day? A lot, as it seems. And how many more depressed people around the world until something changes? I personally think it will not stop any time soon because it is a ripple effect – more negative information means more profit for media companies, more negative information means more depressed people, more depressed people mean more depression medications taken every day, and more medications consequently bring more profit for pharmaceutical companies. And so, it goes. One vicious circle, and we are surely trapped in it.

What would happen to the world if we all stopped spending money?

"Economics has never been a science - and it is even less now than a few years ago."
– PAUL SAMUELSON

I outlined this question sometime in 2018, late in the evening, as I was thinking about how fragile this society is and how everything functions solely based on the principle of people constantly buying new things. And so, the curious idea came up in my head - what would happen if we just stopped buying non-essential stuff for an extended period? Obviously, we unwillingly received part of an answer to this question in 2020 with the coronavirus pandemic since society almost completely stopped. Okay, to be fair, not everything stopped – we still had the chance to buy groceries, and most online shops worked just fine. Amazon (and similar companies) even profited from lockdown. But what would really happen if the majority of people stopped buying everything except the necessary food for some time? In short, economies would probably collapse, many people would lose jobs, and the ripple effect would continue in all industries and aspects of society as we know it. But let's dig deeper into potential consequences for society and what could be changed in this predominantly materialistic world, which is on a constant shopping spree.

Let's imagine a scenario that by some agreement or revolution majority of people around the world jointly decide that they will stop shopping for all non-essential things. In the first couple of days, things would become slightly weird. You would see no one strolling pointlessly around shopping centers. Clothing stores would be empty, tech shops would be empty, and people would go out more to socialize. By week two, most politicians, store owners, and Jeff Bezos would become very stressed and worried. Different media companies and streaming services would also become very anxious. I mean, Netflix surely fits into a category of non-essential things (or services). Results of zero Netflix usage equals even more people in nature, on the streets, socializing with each other. All good so far, for the most part. However, progressing into the second and then third week of decreased compulsive buying, many store owners would start to think about laying off some of their employees who are basically doing nothing all day. We're just at the beginning, and most consequences for current society are just starting to show on the surface.

But what about the overall economy on a global scale? First, let's see how much on average is being spent on food which is for sure essential spending. According to the US Department of Agriculture (USDA), Americans spend around 6.4% of their income on food. In different countries, those percentages are very different, but the general rule is – more developed the country, the less percentage of their income is spent on food. Actually, per World Economic Forum data, there are only eight countries in the world that spend less than 10% of their income on food. Those are Austria (9.9%), Ireland (9.6%), Switzerland (8.7%), UK (8.2%), Canada (9,1%), Singapore (6.7%), Australia (9.8%) and US with beforementioned 6.4%. On the other hand, there are many countries which spend much more on food. Nigeria spends over half of its household income on food, and there are nine other countries that spend over 40% on food. Four of them are in Africa: Nigeria (56.4%), Kenya (46.7%), Cameroon (45.6%), and Algeria (42.5%). Four are in Asia: Kazakhstan (43.0%), Philippines (41.9%), Pakistan (40.9%), and Azerbaijan (40.1%).

Based on that, we can take a ballpark number and say that usually, on a worldwide level, households are spending around 20% on food. It could be less; it could be more, but it is not very relevant for this argument. What is relevant is that if everyone stops spending money on non-essential things, there would be at least 50% of money missing in the system. Consequently, there would be less money taken by government taxes, less revenue for many companies, less profit, and a really big impact on every country's GDP. In that manner, let's pretend that overall yearly spending in the world is 100 trillion dollars. If 20 trillion is being spent on food and an additional 20 on housing, then around 60 trillion is saved in this hypothetical scenario. That means these 60 trillion is missing from the spending part of the economic system. That's very significant. Just imagine if all people decided to put that saved money in the bank. It is clear that banks would go bankrupt. Why? Well, because banks rely on a system where most people are spending more than they earn, and thus they go into debt, and we all know that banks earn money when they have many clients who are in debt. In this reverse case, banks would need to give interest money to clients and not vice versa. Then, of course, banks would declare that interests are going to become negative, which should, in turn, trigger people to start spending those savings.

However, in our imaginary scenario, all people decided that they would not spend their money on unnecessary things under any circumstances. So, the problem becomes even bigger. Banks are on their knees. None of their historic strategies work anymore – people are stubborn, and they refuse to spend. What would happen next? Well, after a prolonged period of time, many people in every industry except food would lose their job. Then the riots would start as those people would spend their savings, and then they would not be able to buy even food. Then, in turn, some of the jobs in the food industry would also be lost. And so it goes. You can probably imagine that there would be wars on the streets.

But there is one big IF here. Maybe people would decide to start living self-sustainable life, meaning they produce everything they need. Because for a happy life we really don't need a new iPhone, nor do we need to travel every month to the new destination. Maybe if that thought were seeded in enough people, then just maybe this new system of slightly less spending would work. And then perhaps we would discover that we're much more than simple spenders and consumers, and we would rely more on discovering ourselves and our meaning in this world because we could all agree that the majority of things we buy are only distractions from discovering our true self. This is in some way romantic and utopian contemplation from my side, but I really think that people are meant to do more than work all day and then spend hard-earned money on new shiny things which are irrelevant in a couple of months. This is the endless circle which doesn't stop ever. The more money you earn, the more gadgets you want. This is called lifestyle inflation. And in a very simplistic manner, this is how our economies around the world are still running like clockwork even though everybody is in debt to everyone else. Basically, it's like a pile of cards on the verge of collapsing, and the only glue keeping everything together is the masses of people buying new things every day.

Are news, movies, and music videos shaping human behavior?

"Whoever controls the media, controls the mind."
– JIM MORRISON

Think about your own thoughts for a moment. How much are those thoughts and behaviors shaped by what you watch, what you read, and what you hear on a daily basis? Seems like we're all different; we all have our own thoughts, we are all unique, and our beliefs are unique. But are they really? Are we really?

From the day we are born, we are influenced by our parents, by our friends, and by everything we read, see, or hear. Parental influence is a whole different story as media also influences them, and thus, they pass their potential nonsense to their children. Parental influence is perhaps best described by using the example of musical influence. Let's say your parents listen to jazz all the time, they also like Tom Waits, Leonard Cohen, and similar artists, then probably child would also have good and similar taste in music. Of course, there is a phrase "*De gustibus non est disputandum*," meaning that people should not argue about tastes. Still, I am sure we can all agree that Tom Waits, Chet Baker, and Bob Dylan represent better music taste than that of Cardi B or Miley Cyrus. So, music that influenced your parents will probably directly influence your taste in music. And your taste in music will influence many other things in your life like your friends, your community, your topics of interest, et cetera. Now, this is only one example of parents' influence. There many others, like your beliefs, career choice, and political identification. So, as mentioned, parents are also influenced by what they listen to, what they watch on television, and of course what their parents taught them. And so it goes.

However, this is only the tip of the iceberg, especially in modern times. Children are more than ever influenced by media, as they can now consume information all the time from every device, 24/7. One would say yes, but they have a choice on what they read, watch, or listen to. And one would be massively wrong. Namely, almost all information presented to children (or adults, for that matter) is what the main publishers and media companies want you to see. Of course, you can find information from different sources, but that takes a lot of effort, and so the majority of people (and I mean 90+ percent) consume only content that is presented to them in the most convenient way. That is mainstream television media, top 10 search results on Google, and top news articles. Rarely anyone goes beyond 1st page on Google, and whatever you write in Google as a search term, you will get top 10 results from leading mainstream media & news companies like BBC, NY Times, and similar. That is staggering, isn't it? I mean, if you are curious, you would need to spend endless hours searching for articles/videos containing different narratives than it is served to you as mainstream. Many who are curious give up. It's that hard. Where does that lead humanity in means of consuming information which then leads to defining how you think, who you are, what are your beliefs, and everything else for that matter? Well, it leads to narrow-mindedness in many cases! Having that in mind, let's look at the example of the United States of America and where is most of the news coming from.

Basically, in today's world, people have the illusion of choice when it comes to searching and consuming information. Many people think they are getting their information from hundreds of sources. While in reality, media has never been more consolidated. Six media giants in the US now control a staggering 90% of what we read, watch or listen to. So, let's look at more details into that matter; it's rather important.

In the last decades, media companies have been merging more than ever, and big conglomerates are controlling more and more information. In the 1980s, there were more than 50 corporations that provided news (and all other publications and media, including books, radio, and television) to the American people. In the 1990s, that number dropped a lot. By around 50%, to be more specific. Fast forward to a new millennium, and we only have a few corporations that completely dominate the media and publishing industry: Comcast, AT&T (owns Warner Media), and Viacom. They (almost) own everything. You name it; CNN, NBC, ABC, Disney, HBO, Cinemax, Sky Group, Warner Bros... Nearly everyone in the world is familiar with those names as their impact goes far outside USA borders. They are basically responsible for a significant amount of news being shared in the West. There are, of course, other big news companies that are not controlled by the abovementioned conglomerates. Think of New York Times, Chicago Tribune, or perhaps Los Angeles Times. There are more, of course, but the point here is that they are also somehow under the direct or indirect impact of the conglomerate machine. Ben Bagdikian, Pulitzer Prize-winning journalist, former Dean of the Graduate School of Journalism at UC Berkeley, and author of The New Media Monopoly, portrays the media giants as a "cartel" that has enough influence to change U.S. politics and define social values.

And what about Internet? Well, In the beginning, the Internet was the platform for free thinkers, adopted as a liberating force from corporate-owned media. However, over time, large new sites and platforms on Internet also became part of large media conglomerates. Roughly 80% of the top 20 online news sites in the US are owned by large media companies. Then we have Facebook, Twitter, and Google, who at first celebrated freedom of speech, but recently they are pushing the narrative only from a handful of big media corporations, and additionally, they embrace censorship more with each passing day.

So what, one would think? Well, what we should be most concerned about, is the narrowing of choices because that removes the full spectrum of views and information from people with how to behave, what to think, and how to choose its government. This dangerous trend threatens self-thinking and democracy itself. So, where does it all lead if our opinions are influenced by a few conglomerates? Well, it surely does not lead to curiosity, prosperity, and critical thinking. And the latter is most important as people who are thinkers and who question media, movies, documentaries, news, and governments are not really loved in this world nor by governments nor by media corporations. Who needs critical thinkers, ha? A liberal and diverse world needs them, I would say.

So based on that, let's look at a couple of examples and studies about mass media and how they can influence people both on psychological and physical levels. Namely, many recent studies suggest that the news can affect us in surprising ways – from our perception of danger and risk to the content of our dreams to our chances of having a heart attack. Depending on what we watch, listen, and read, media can have a significant impact on our lives. From our opinion of different political leaders, how we perceive pandemic to the beforementioned content of our dreams – news is sneaking into our subconscious and thus affect our lives profoundly. Some people can even develop post-traumatic stress disorder because of negative news. Not to mention anxiety and other psychological effects that news can have on us. One article published in the International Journal of behavioral medicine by Attila Szabo, Katey L. Hopkinson, describes this very well:

"The psychological effects of televised news were studied in 2 groups (n = 179) of undergraduate students who watched a 15-min random newscast followed by either a 15-min progressive relaxation exercise or a 15-min lecture (control condition). Subjective measures of state anxiety, total mood disturbance (TMD), positive affect, and negative affect were obtained before and after the news, as well as following relaxation exercise or the lecture. The results show that state anxiety and TMD

increased, whereas positive affect decreased in both groups after watching the news, and 15 min later, they returned to baseline (pre-news) only in the relaxation group, whereas they remained unchanged in the control group. These findings demonstrate that watching the news on television triggers persisting negative psychological feelings that could not be buffered by attention-diverting distraction (i.e., lecture), but only by a directed psychological intervention such as progressive relaxation."

Isn't that something, ha? Especially if we know that majority of media served to us is controlled by a few corporations. What do you think is happening in high-level meetings in those corporations? No, they are not thinking about how to bring you the most relevant and most important news for your wellbeing. They are talking about how to publish news or information that will bring them more revenue. Now, of course, from time to time, they will bring relevant news and important articles, but in the majority of situations, they will try to make money out of gibberish news they serve to all of us.

So, just stop for a minute and think about the type of news you're receiving every day, all day. Is that news positive or negative? Primarily negative, and this is on purpose. Why might you ask? Well, simply because negative news (and movies, for that matter) will receive more clicks and more views which then makes more money for corporations that makes the news. There's psychology research in there. Not that they just decided – "Ok, let's play negative news to people and see what'll happen." They did just the opposite – used different studies in people's desires and behaviors to their advantage. There are many studies around there on why people read negative news, and some news companies even did experiments on their own websites. A good example here is the news site City Reporter, as they did the experiment for one day to see what will happen if they only share positive news. They placed several negative articles, but they rearranged wording and sentences so that even those sounded more positive. Results? In that one day, they had around 70% fewer readers.

Then we have some more serious research that happened with an actual scientific approach. Researchers Stuart Soroka and Marc Trussler from McGill University in Canada run an experiment to measure what their volunteers actually read and what they say they would like to read. To keep the story short – they used cameras and measurement devices to analyze the eye movements of experiment participants when they read stories they offered to them. There were various stories on the same page, and participants were asked to really read stories they wanted to read, but they didn't know they were monitored and that their eye movement was monitored. At the end of the experiment, they were asked what kind of stories they usually preferred. Most answered that they usually like positive stories and that, in fact, they think that news is constantly focused on negative stories. And what was the actual experiment result? Well, I think everyone can guess by now. Almost everyone actually read negative stories and articles even though they were offered a mix of positive, neutral, and negative stories and articles.

Now, this is intriguing, isn't it? People subconsciously prefer good and positive news but choose negative ones, which then negatively affect them both psychologically and physically. This is the story of modern times, unfortunately. So, what do you think will happen in future years? Well, we see that now already. Have you watched popular music videos recently? They are all shaping young people to the degrees of biological and physical changes. The main propaganda in music videos is one part of the (female) body and how to shake it constantly. Consequently, so many young (and also older) people are now obsessed with this new model for beauty. Not that I have anything against it, but I just wanted to prove the point how just one part of media (popular music videos) can influence some parts of society.

Now think about how all those music videos, movies, and news shape your psyche if we can see the pure fact of changes in even physical appearance. It is weird in some ways for sure, and it will become even more obvious (and probably weirder) in the coming years. Media will have more control, and media will shape even more opinions, especially for young people who are growing up with screens all around them from their birth.

"If you don't read the newspaper, you're uninformed. If you read the newspaper, you're misinformed."
- MARK TWAIN

What would happen if there was a limit to a maximum amount of wealth per person?

"Earth provides enough to satisfy every man's needs, but not every man's greed."
– MAHATMA GANDHI

Imagine a world where the maximum amount of money and wealth anyone on Earth can have is capped at 100 million dollars. What would change in that kind of world? How would that world function? Would it be better, or would it collapse? Those are all questions I will try to answer in this chapter.

This subject concerned me for quite some time. Constantly in today's world, we are bombarded with news about the success of multi-billionaires. They are modern-day heroes, they know everything, they are someone modern generations should look up to, and they are represented (in many cases) as saviors of the world. But should they be celebrated like that? Are they really modern-day heroes, or are they just hungry for more money and more power? And would they still be like that if they couldn't earn more than 100 million dollars at any point in time? What would then drive them?

Wealth has always been something everyone desires. From ancient times to today, the wealthiest people always had significant power, and they always wanted even more. No society in history made a conscious decision to set up a limit on maximum wealth per person. Ok, to be fair, there is a maximum wage limit in Cuba currently, but that's another story with a completely different implementation.

So, let's think about what would happen in that scenario of limited wealth around the world. Say someone earns 100 million dollars and then he/she receives a phone call from the Ministry of Wealth Control (MWC), and they say:

"Congratulations, you won The Game of Capitalism. You'll get a winning plate, and everything you earn from now on will go to charity."

- Day 1 of limit law. Nothing happens except the media goes to outrage. Stocks fall worldwide.

- On day 2, the news really struck down, especially on wealthy people. Many standard people look positive at the news, but they are worried about what will happen.

- Day 10 – news is bombarded every day with newly introduced law, and social unrest can be seen worldwide.

For now, let's stop with day-by-day counting. However, the potential consequences could be seen clearly. Namely, in the current world, limiting wealth would probably not result in a positive situation. This change would probably result in positive progress in the world in the long term; however, with the current establishment, so many billionaires, and twisted definition of value and progress in society, the decision to limit individual wealth would conclude with unimaginable negative results for many years. In 100 years, society would perhaps be better; however, for 1st generation, it would be devastating. Why devastating, one could ask? Well, because society as a whole and its values need to change completely to adopt the limited wealth idea. Basically, the whole generation (and probably more) is needed to conclude its chapter before you can introduce a new set of values, even if you are changing only one thing (but an important one) such as the amount of money any individual can have. Having said that, let's try to imagine what would happen in different industries and in people's lives.

- Tech industry:

I would say that this is a category that would probably be highly impacted. Namely, we could expect many newer things that keep coming out, such as new smartphones, new tablets, and new devices, to dry up and slow down considerably. This is a rather fast industry, and while there are, of course, many people in the industry doing things for a better world, many are also there only for the money. So, if society put a cap on that money, well, then probably not so many hours would be spent on managing those businesses and inventing new things. Now, don't get me wrong, it would not happen in every company, but let's be realistic; many people are driven only by money, and they would not do the same thing if money was capped.

Say that owner of a big IT company reaches 100M$ and he/she/they cannot earn anymore. Would they still pursue the same "rat race," or would they settle down and spend time on perhaps more meaningful things like traveling the world, spending time in nature and with their family, and helping people in need? No one knows but looking at the current society, I would say that after the introduction of the limit law, in the first 100 years, a significant delay in the production of technology goods would probably happen. And maybe that would be a good thing for society. As one smart person once said, *"People need to be wise enough to decide not to make some technological progress or product even though they have knowledge and ability to do so."* A lot of people are now saying that social networks are destroying the sole fabric of society as we know it. And there are many such examples. Do you think those products would be built if their CEOs, early investors, and many others were limited to how much they could gain for supporting or inventing them? Probably not, but time will tell.

- Food Industry

Innovation and the extreme wealth of individuals in the food industry are not as common as in the tech industry, and thus, I would say changes would not be as dramatic. Food would still be produced; however, probably the biggest food producers would reduce their processing plants significantly. This would probably result in an additional number of smaller food producers, which is for sure a good thing.

- Education

There aren't many billionaires in the education industry; however, there are some. Bertil Hult, the 75-year-old founder of EF Education First, is worth $5 billion and is among the world's richest college dropouts. He founded his business, which originally focused on organizing summer trips to the UK so his fellow Swedish students could learn English in the basement of his dorm (apparently). Sunny Varkey is another billionaire in education. He is worth $2 billion, and he founded GEMS Education. According to Forbes, the company operates 50 private K-12 schools enrolling around 140,000 students worldwide, with its first U.S. school located in Chicago. There are only a few more billionaires in education, but I will not comment on all of them as it is not so important for the topic. Namely, one can conclude that education would not be changed much if the wealth limit rule was enforced. One thing that would change for sure is the education curriculum in some way since ultra-wealthy individuals influence education from early times. One good example of that is John D. Rockefeller. Basically, he influenced many categories in the education system by enforcing learning programs where he could benefit from thousands of "educated" learners for his factories and industries. One could say that this kind of educational system was designed to keep us uneducated and docile. This is another topic, but it is related to this one because if the wealth limit was enforced, then we wouldn't have those uber-wealthy people who have so much power that they can influence the education systems.

- Auto industry

Oh well, here we could expect a lot of changes when the wealth limit system is introduced. Namely, in the car industry, there are a significant amount of very wealthy people who are shaping the industry. Let's just name a few.

Did you know that siblings Susanne Klatten and

Stefan Quandt own almost half of BMW? Susanne Hanna Ursula Klatten is a German billionaire heiress, and her net worth is estimated at 23.2 billion US dollars, ranking her the richest woman in Germany and the 50th richest person in the world, according to Forbes. Siblings are descendants of Guenther Quandt, who built a German industrial empire by, among other things, supplying weapons to the Nazis during World War II. In the years since the family has secured stakes in both Daimler-Benz AG and BMW.

Also, did you know that Bill Gates can also be on this list? How? Well, everybody knows that he is a billionaire, but rare people know that he also invested a good amount of money in AutoNation Inc., and his stake is worth around 1 billion dollars. Then, of course, we have Elon Musk, with his huge wealth coming from Tesla. And there are many, many other billionaires and multi-hundred millionaires either directly or indirectly (via stock ownership or similar) tied to the automotive industry.

One can only assume what would happen with all those innovations and products that are coming from the automotive industry if there wasn't the possibility to earn colossal wealth. Would Tesla exist now, would we have an electric car renaissance? Well, no one knows, but I would say progress in the industry would follow a different stream than it is now.

- Real-estate

This is a rather specific industry in a way that there is a huge number of local 'bosses' who are earning a significant amount of money by building apartments and then lending or selling them. However, many of those people have wealth way below 100 million of our imaginative limit, so things would not change for the majority. However, luxurious buildings, huge business offices, and the hotel industry would change for sure as there are a pretty good amount of ultra-rich (over 100 million $) people concerned about their wealth in this segment. Some of the huge international hotels would probably change significantly or even close down. On the positive side, perhaps the prices of some apartments would go down because there would be fewer greedy billionaires.

- Oil & Gas industry

Hm... I think there's no need to spend sentences here as we all know how many billionaires (and perhaps trillionaires) there are in Oil & Gas industry. This industry simply cannot exist without oligarchs from different continents. Enough said. Any speculation of what would happen if their wealth was limited to 100 million dollars could end up in writing stories about the war.

- Pharmaceutical industry

In these times (i.e., coronavirus times and Pharma Gods), similar things would happen as described in the previous paragraph regarding Oil & Gas industry. Somewhat hard to speculate. Perhaps pharma drugs would not be developed, and perhaps we would have (almost) free mushrooms in local pharmacy. In my opinion, in this industry, there shouldn't be anyone earning vast amounts of money, and that drugs that really help human life should be made available for everyone relatively cheap.

In the end, we can for sure conclude that limited wealth for individuals would include a huge number of changes in society and in different industries. Those changes would for sure (at least in the beginning) decrease the number of innovations in many industries. For ordinary people, many things would probably stay the same or maybe even improve. Because let's face it – we don't need huge amounts of new products which are being introduced to the market every day, solely because new products bring massive revenue to companies and their owners. However, in my humble opinion, after a couple of decades, society would change for the better, and money streams would turn into more compassion between people and not into more greed as it is currently in many situations.

How was the education system created and where it's heading?

"Education is what remains after one has forgotten everything he learned in school. It is a miracle that curiosity survives formal education."
– ALBERT EINSTEIN

Have you ever thought about education system history? How did it all start, and how it's going? What was the purpose? What are you exactly doing inside that system? Who first decided that we needed a formal education system? Were those people sitting at the round table and determining the direction of humanity with the education system? When you think about it, a lot of questions come to mind. Here I'll try to think about all those questions and then some more, both from a historical and conspiratorial perspective. Also, I'll dig into the beginnings of education in ancient times to where we are now. You may think, ok, but that's all in different history books. And you could be right; however, we also sometimes need to question history books as they are part of the standard and official education per se, and we know that official education is many times changed to conform to the current political narrative. So, it's all part of the same system, any way you look at it. And that's why I think it is essential to look around for different clues around the education system, its beginnings, and its purpose.

Before going more deeply into the education system, we first need to distinguish formal education from informal education. Namely, informal education was present in human history for thousands of years. Rich people of that time had some kind of formal and informal education, but it was not enforced on them (except by their parents.) Think about Egyptian Pharaohs, their parents, and their children. What exactly were they teaching their children, and from where did that part of education come from? That's almost impossible to know as many texts from that time are either not discovered, those discovered are uninterpretable, and many are destroyed (on purpose or accidentally, nobody knows).

As it is (in its original natural form), education existed from the beginning of humans and animals. Adults have innate and genetic intuition that they would like to transfer the knowledge they acquired to their young ones. Sometimes that's a good thing, and sometimes that's a bad thing mainly because nowadays we have so many unconscious people walking on this Earth trying to pass their "knowledge" to their children. And if the knowledge they acquired is not accurate or without any meaning, well, then it will be even more spurious when it is passed on to their children. That's how generations of people are developed to believe complete nonsense with their whole being.

On the other hand, when thinking about the official history of education and knowledge, one of the first things that come to mind is Alexandria's Library, built in the 3rd century BCE. This library, of course, didn't function as today's formal education. There weren't schools, classes, or standard teachers as we know them today. Everything was completely different. So, how did we arrive in today's world where we have many public and private schools, which are controlled by either governments, companies, or individuals?

Think about the following – how are all ideas and projects realized in history? Mostly by trying and failing. Child education can be seen as a project that has been tested in many different forms in society's history. Not that variations and try-and-fail methods are bad *per se,* but in this case, variations were not done to come up with the best solution for people as it seems. Variations were done to come up with the best solution so that at the end of the formal education, the system yields the exact kind of adult people who are needed to satisfy the current needs of the particular economic system. Having that in mind and concerning the biological history of our species, schools are very recent institutions. And this is in some way self-explanatory because, as we learned, education or schooling produces the kind of people needed for that era. When we were first hunters and gatherers, children learned different things by watching their parents' lives. On a side note here - anthropologists have reported that the hunter-gatherer communities they researched did not distinguish between work and play as almost all of life was understood as some kind of play. Then we transitioned to agricultural and industrial society. And then everything changed, at least from the perspective of formal education but also from many other vital perspectives of one's life.

Agricultural development severely impacted people's lives. Families started having more children who were required to work in the fields. Those children needed to learn specific skills from their parents. Additionally, during the development of agriculture, hierarchies started to become a real thing. On top of that, the main lessons that children had to learn were suppression of their own will, obedience, a show of respect, and fear toward the ones in power and control.

Fast forward to an industrial society, and lessons about obedience and fear became an even more important part of children's daily lives (and adults). Prominent employers in the industry wanted to create efficient workers, and one way to do that was (and still is) schooling. Big oil oligarchs like Rockefellers played a significant game here. Countries and governments then followed a similar example.

In the 19th and 20th centuries, schooling became more traditional and part of every child's ordinary life and basically everyone. However, one thing did not change significantly, and that is how education remained very shortsighted as children were thought mainly to use only one part of their brain (which is needed for current businesses and industry). In contrast, the second part of the brain primarily remained untouched. Also, one of the most important flaws of the education system remained, and that is how children are not taught to ask questions but mainly to follow the system. Touching on that topic opens another one that relates to old Prussia (Germany) and their psychological research of potential education systems for children. Here we're getting a bit into the conspiratorial field but bear with me, as I think it is important for context.

Let's start with the philosophy of John Locke's view (1690) that children are a blank slate and lessons from

Jean-Jacques Rousseau's opinion that bad behavior is a product of learning and socialization. Following that logic, some would think if children were blank slates, then there is a possibility (and perhaps need?) to program that blank slate. Partly based on that predicament (*without going into details as it would take the whole book*), Prussia established a three-tiered educational system. Essentially, by some opinions, the system was about thought control and how to basically "program" young minds. In one way, the plan was to keep children in the general population from reading or learning with context during their early years. The keyword here is "general population," as children with rich and powerful parents didn't go to public schools at all.

Basically, by some opinions, it seems like Prussians established this three-tier system in order to achieve particular results in different categories of young people. In the lowest category, called *volksschule*, they were using the method to divide whole ideas and disciplines into different subjects, which were then again divided into different units in the period of time during the day (sounds like standard school?). With that kind of approach, with all those divisions and a mixture of topics, no one actually knew what was really happening in the world or in any specific field for that matter.

Children knew the facts, but they didn't know much more than that. With that approach, children's blank slates were filled with a mixture of facts that are not essential for their true development. It was a fundamentally simple method of knowledge suppression in some way. Because you learn something, but in reality, you don't. And many started to hate learning as it is during the process. That's the real problem because learning should be something fun and interesting. Nevertheless, this model remained and was replicated in other countries.

Namely, in 1814, one American citizen, Edward Everett, went to Prussia to get his Ph.D. Edward Everett later came to be governor of Massachusetts. Apparently, he was spreading the word in the USA quickly since, after him, many influential Americans came to Germany to earn their degrees. Among them was Horace Mann, who traveled to Germany to investigate how the educational process worked. Upon return, he was one of the main people responsible for Education Reform in the USA. Many people that returned from Germany were appointed to major universities in the USA, spreading the models similar to the Prussian education system. Basically, many universities started to promote the concept that "the state is the father of children," among others. Now imagine if young people are instructed from their early beginnings that the state is their father in some way. Those children are then mostly feared by the state. And fear means control. Hereby don't get me wrong, as many good things also came from the structure of that kind of education system but perhaps it could have been built better to serve curious young minds.

Now, all of this sounds conspiratorial. And in some ways, it is. But it paints the picture that perhaps formal structured education was not here (at least in the beginning) just to teach our young ones the best possible things. It was designed to produce "soldiers" for the economic system of that time. Is it different today? In some ways, it is, but still, we see so much nonsense in schools and universities. The majority of people coming out of universities of any kind can't remember anything they "learned" during their 5-year period of attendance. Societies should make a practical joke of that situation by asking the same people to take various exams five years later. Everyone would fail. Even those who got the best grades on those exact exams. That's because many things being thought are not something people could really use in their personal or professional lives.

It is becoming more and more certain that formal education of today is a relic of history that is still being enforced as the best method to have a good career. Actually, it is far from reality and will disappear or change completely in the coming years. Whether it will disappear in 20 years or 100, it doesn't matter, but it will for sure. I mean, can you imagine people in 2200 going to standard schools? No, for sure not. Education as we know it is on the verge of becoming something completely different. And rightly so. It held its position long enough now. Almost everything changed, and education mostly didn't, while education should be the first thing to change as it represents the first stepping stone into what little brains think and want to become in their lives.

How would people behave if there were no laws?

"Laws are like sausages, it is better not to see them being made."
– OTTO VON BISMARCK

This question has always been somewhere in the back of my mind. Mostly because I sometimes like to dream that we're all intelligent and altruistic beings who could organize themselves without the need for some written and enforced laws. Then again, looking at how people behave, I understand that my dream is just that – a dream that cannot be fulfilled in current society.

Quoting George Carlin, *"Think of how stupid the average person is, and realize half of them are stupider than that,"* it should be clear why we cannot have a lawless society, at least not yet (and perhaps never). Nevertheless, let's indulge ourselves and hypothesize how could lawless society look like and perhaps romanticize how it would look if we were all wise enough so that we don't need laws at all.

By many popular opinions, a society without laws would be a society in a state of almost constant chaos. A state without laws and government would probably look like some type of anarchy. By the Merriam-Webster dictionary, anarchy is a state of lawlessness or political disorder due to the absence of governmental authority and rules. Life without some type of rules to control us would be a state of disorder by many opinions. Mine included as elaborated briefly in the first paragraph. However, before going deeper into how that kind of society would look like, let's use history as a teacher and see how laws developed in different cultures.

In prehistoric times there weren't many laws. Ancient people lived in small groups where they were defining their own laws if those could be called laws. As societies grew so the laws became more detailed, and there were more of them. One of the basic and most important laws and rules for every society is the law about murder. In early societies, the implication of murder law was not implemented via the legal system but by blood revenge. Additionally, early societies had some forms of payment that could be made instead of blood revenge. For example, early Germanic society had *weregild* (man price). It represented the possibility to repay the victim's family instead of blood revenge. The amount of *weregild* was calculated by a person's status in society. The wergild of a woman was usually equal to, and often more than, that of a man of the same class.

Then we also have early Sumerian codes and rules. Sumerian Code of Ur-Nammu represents one of the oldest codes where some kind of prohibitions against murder appears. The code states, "If a man commits a murder, that man must be killed." Pretty simple, isn't it. Furthermore, in the Ten Commandments given by God to Moses, it is explicitly stated that "Thou shalt not kill."

In Islam, according to the Qur'an, one of the biggest sins is to kill another human being who has committed no fault. *"For that cause, we decreed for the Children of Israel that whosoever killed a human being for other than manslaughter or corruption in the earth, it shall be as if he had killed all mankind, and whoso saveth the life of one, it shall be as if he had saved the life of all mankind.* [Quran verse 5:32]

Murder was one of the earliest "laws" passed on to society, but it wasn't the only one. During the time, codes and laws became more detailed. Ur-Nammu, the Sumerian ruler, created the first law code that consisted of casuistic statements such as "if...then..." Then we also have the Code of Hammurabi. Probably everyone remembers that one from school. It is three centuries younger than the beforementioned Code of Ur-Nammu. The Code of Hammurabi was probably the earliest and most complete legal code ever written. Code consisted of 282 rules. Those rules described commercial interactions and different fines and punishments. Interestingly enough, code was carved into massive, finger-shaped black stone. Across centuries many things happened to that stone, but it was finally rediscovered in 1901. Today it resides in the Louvre Museum.

Those examples are only the beginnings of laws in our world, but during the course of hundreds (and thousands) years, laws started to shape every possible part of human and non-human behavior. Every aspect of society now has thousands and thousands of laws, and that is surely a good thing in one aspect. Yet in another, some laws are rather complex, some are only there to protect and serve those who created them, and some are simply weird. The latter kinds are always the most interesting ones, so let's just name a few:

- In Arizona, it is against the law to have a sleeping donkey in your bathtub after 7 p.m.
- It's illegal to hike naked in Switzerland.
- It's illegal to wear high heels to the Acropolis.
- It is illegal to chew gum in Singapore.
- Interestingly, it is illegal to drive blindfolded in Alabama (*as it should be*).
- If you own any chickens in Quitman, Georgia, it is illegal to let them cross the road.
- In Florida, it is illegal to pass wind in a public place after 6 p.m. on Thursdays.
- In Scotland, if someone knocks on your door and requires the use of your toilet, you must let them enter.
- In Samoa, it is illegal to forget your wife's birthday.
- In California, it's illegal to whistle for a lost canary before 7 a.m.
- In Colorado, it's illegal to keep a couch on your porch.
- In Delaware, you can't sell dog hair.
- It's illegal to ride a cow drunk in Scotland.

- It's illegal to wear a mask in public in Denmark (*this will probably change in today's mask madness all around the world*).
- It's illegal to swear in the U.A.E.
- It's illegal to wear lacy undies in Russia.
- It's unlawful to build a sandcastle in Spain.
- In Georgia, it's illegal to live on a boat for more than 30 days.
- In Hawaii, it's illegal to place a coin in one's ear.
- In Illinois, it's legal for underage culinary students to drink alcohol.
- In Indiana, it's illegal to ride a horse above 10 Mph.
- It's illegal to reincarnate without permission in China.
- It's illegal to kill bigfoot in British Columbia, Canada.
- It's illegal to pee in the ocean in Portugal.
- In Kentucky, a woman cannot marry the same man four times. *Hm... Why would she?*
- In Maryland, sleeveless shirts are banned in public parks.
- **Worldwide in 2020 and 2021, it is illegal to breathe unobstructed air!**

Ok, the last one is a joke — sort of.

So clearly, there are thousands and thousands of laws written during the course of a long history with the goal to somehow control or shape human behavior and all processes related to almost everything in the world. And as we also determined - this is mostly good, at least with humanity at the current level of (im)maturity. So, let's see how society would function without laws and rules.

A good place to start imagining how society would function is to remove important laws and rules such as those related to murder. Per Cornell law, murder is defined as killing another human being with malice aforethought. Malice aforethought is a legal term of art that encompasses the following types of murder: "Intent-to-kill murder," "Grievous-bodily-harm murder" - killing someone in an attack intended to cause them grievous bodily harm. As we know, all across the world, there are laws that basically say one should not kill another person, and if it does happen, there will be dire consequences. So, if we remove those dire consequences written in different laws, well, then we would have big problems on the streets almost immediately. Therefore, let's imagine what would happen if only 1 law (about murder) is cancelled:

- Day 1 – Governments around the world remove all laws related to murder.

- Day 2 – A lot of people around the world start killing other people as there are no consequences anymore. What do I mean by "a lot"? Well, according to some estimates, psychopathy is found in about one percent of the general population, and for reasons that are poorly understood, most psychopaths are male. Now, not all psychopaths are criminals, and not all psychopaths will have the urge to kill someone. However, in these circumstances where there are no consequences for killing, we can freely guess that some normal people would also do the bad deed either for revenge, for food, or for whatever other reason. So, we can play with numbers, but I would say that 1 percent of people who would immediately start killing is an understatement but let's go with it. Having said that, with a current human population of 7,8 Billion, we would have 78 000 000 (78 million) people wandering around looking for someone to kill.

- Day 3 – All-around chaos is on the streets. Rich people are going in bunkers.

- Day 4 – Army is being sent on the streets. Every country is approaching civil war.

- Day 5 – People stop working or going to work as they are afraid.

- Day 6 – Shortage of guns and ammunition in gun stores.

- Day 7 – Normal people are doing everything they can to secure their homes. Meaning they get aggressive and full of arms too.

- Day 8 – Complete anarchy.

And so on, and so on...

Perchance I am exaggerating, but perhaps I am not. Possibly the consequences would be even more dreadful and happen even more quickly. Remember, this is by removing only one law. Of course, this is one of the most important laws but, nevertheless. In that case, let's imagine what would happen if we, for example, remove laws related to sexual assaults? The collapse of society could happen even more quickly. Keep in mind, humans are sexual beings, and while this is terrific because of all the pleasure sexuality gives us, some people cannot really control their voluptuous desires. And the only thing that is keeping some people from committing different sexual assaults are laws that will put them in prison for life if they decide to be "nasty." Based on that predicament, let's look at some of the current statistics where laws and punishments are still present and valid:

- Per National Sexual Violence Resource Center, nearly 1 in 5 women (18.3%) and 1 in 71 men (1.4%) in the United States have been raped at some time in their lives, including completed forced penetration, attempted forced penetration, or alcohol/drug-facilitated completed penetration.

- A United Nations statistical report compiled from government sources revealed that more than 250,000 cases of rape or attempted rape were recorded by police annually. The reported data covered 65 countries. This report did not include South Africa having 50,000 rapes per year or some other countries with high rape statistics, such as Egypt.

- Per data from Unwoman.org, at least 155 countries have passed laws on domestic violence, and 140 have laws on sexual harassment in the workplace. However, even when laws exist, this does not mean they are always compliant with international standards and recommendations or are implemented and enforced.

- CDC data shows that approximately 1 in 21 men (4.8%) reported that they were made to penetrate someone else during their lifetime; most men who were made to penetrate someone else reported that the perpetrator was either an intimate partner (44.8%) or an acquaintance (44.7%).

- An estimated 13% of women and 6% of men have experienced sexual coercion in their lifetime (i.e., unwanted sexual penetration after being pressured in a nonphysical way); and 27.2% of women and 11.7% of men have experienced unwanted sexual contact.

- Most female victims of completed rape (79.6%) experienced their first rape before the age of 25; 42.2% experienced their first completed rape before the age of 18 years.

- More than one-quarter of male victims of completed rape (27.8%) experienced their first rape when they were ten years of age or younger.

- National sexual violence resource center (NSVRC) estimates that 734,630 people were raped (threatened, attempted, or completed) in the United States in 2018.

- Per US National sexual violence resource center, approximately 1 in 6 women (16.1% or an estimated 19.2 million women) and approximately 1 in 10 men (9.6% or an estimated 10.6 million men) experienced sexual coercion (e.g., being worn down by someone who repeatedly asked for sex, sexual pressure due to someone using their influence or authority) at some point in their lifetime.

There could be materials on this kind of statistics for dozens of books; however, I just wanted to make a point that even though there are thorough laws and punishments with regards to any kinds of sexual assaults, they are still happening. And not in small numbers but in millions. Now imagine how much that number would grow without laws. One thing is for sure – a woman walking on the street would not feel safe. Of course, many, many people would behave the same with or without laws, and they would help any victim but believe me, there would be so many people raping anything and anyone they could find. All day, every day. That would completely destabilize society. So, we're back to square one as we were with murder law abolishment. That is – complete anarchy on the streets and probably destruction of current society. At least in the first few years. Or decades, probably. I mean, possibly in 30-50 years, people would find ways of behaving without written laws. By that, I don't mean that people would suddenly improve enough and become new Buddhas since for that, we would need hundreds and hundreds of years of a completely different set of values.

Then again, some laws, if removed, would benefit society instantly. Think about taxation laws. Sure, some ways of the government collecting money for public services is needed; however, in many cases, those taxes and means of government using their citizens as sheep who constantly pay money are simply too big. Additionally, many different economic laws, if changed or completely abolished, could benefit society instantly and especially those in need. Many laws are being passed because of lobbying or special interests for the most influential people and entities. Almost never for the poor ones or for average Joe's. Thus, abolishing those laws that only contribute to rich becoming even more rich and poor becoming poorer would profoundly benefit society, especially in a couple of years or decades.

Also, there are laws that are simply absurd in many countries and need to be changed promptly because they serve no one, and in most cases, they actually oppress people. Without those laws, society would live better for sure.

Let's just name a few:

1. Iran's Dress Code

Almost everyone is somehow familiar with this one. This law basically does not allow women to appear in public without Islamic dress (hijab). And if some woman decides to do the opposite, then she risks imprisonment or a fine. This law really doesn't make any sense, and more and more women in Iran are against it. Especially since there is no such law imposed upon men, so it is by itself discriminatory.

2. Ban on women driving in Saudi Arabia

Now, this is a really silly ban, and it's not even a law, but it somehow functions like one. Namely, the Saudi government restricts women from driving by imposing a ban on granting them driving licenses. This ban has many negative consequences for women as it limits their travel and freedom in several ways.

3. Uganda's "Miniskirt Law"

Ugandan government in 2014 signed controversial

"antipornography" legislation which basically outlaws miniskirts. This very strange law describes what kind of clothes are revealing too much and thus restricts women from wearing them in public. Ethics and Integrity Minister Simon Lokodo stated:

"If you dress in such a way that you irritate the mind and excite the people, then you are badly dressed; if you draw the attention of the other person outside there with a malicious purpose of exciting and stimulating him or her into sex."

Again, these kinds of statements and laws limit independence for women in many ways, and it shows how freedoms can also regress in modern times. It is simply amazing how stupid people can be with their behaviours and their laws. Remember that those laws are not just written down one day, and that's that. No. People went into meetings, they had discussions, and then they potentially agreed. Then someone needed to write that down and pass it to congress (depending on the country, of course). Many activities and processes need to happen before any law is passed. So, it is unbelievable that someone would go into such trouble to write a law about miniskirts for women. What is the purpose here? Why would someone even think about it? It is complete insanity, and it is only one example out of hundreds.

Society needs to think about progressing and making laws that would enable progression. Some laws clearly need to be abolished, some need to be changed, and some will need to stay with us almost forever because people are not yet ready to live without rules since the majority is not yet in that state of (mind) development. A perfect society with a different set of values and different human behaviour could potentially live without rules and laws, but we're not even close to that level as humanity. Perhaps in thousands of years, when we understand what is important in life and how not to behave, then we could change societies from law-abiding citizens to conscious and wise citizens.

"Wise men, though all laws were abolished, would lead the same life."

- ARISTOPHANES

Are we all living in our little matrix(es)?

"The matrix is all about boxes. It exists to keep us living in boxes, and thinking in boxes, and doing the same thing everyone else is doing, all day, for the rest of our lives, because boxes, and patterns, and the status quo make humans easy to control."
– SHAMAN DUREK

Matrix is defined as something within or from which something else originates, develops, or takes form. Also, it can be defined as the set of conditions that provides a system in which something grows or develops. There is, of course, a mathematical definition where the matrix is a collection of numbers arranged into a fixed number of rows and columns; however, this one is not of much interest to me with regards to the question in this chapter. And lastly, there is Matrix in popular culture. This is the one that probably came to your mind while reading the question in the headline of this chapter. This idea hypothesizes Matrix-like computer simulation of reality created by more advanced, possibly post-human beings. While this is a rather interesting idea, and I spent numerous hours reading about it, this is not what I was thinking while noting down the question at the beginning of this chapter. Namely, here I would like to express my thoughts when observing day-to-day activities and patterns of human beings during their personal and business lives and how those activities seem like we're all creating our little matrixes, boxes, and boundaries, thus limiting our own human potential.

Most days of almost any human life is basically the same pattern. Let's say you live for 79 years on this planet. Out of those, you spend around 33 years or 12045 days in bed. Sleep counts for 26 years, and the other 7 years are spent trying to sleep, reading a book, or some other activities. The average person spends on work around 13 years and 2 months. Of course, some people work less, some work more, but this is ballpark value for most people. The average human mammal also spends astonishing 11 years and 4 months watching different screens (TV, mobile phone, PC). On eating, we spend around 3 years and 1 month. Romantic activities aren't completely gone yet, as we spend around 395 days practicing them in one way or another. Herby, use your imagination on what activities romance can include.

There is a lot of other statistical data on how we are spending our life, but you get the point. I just wanted to paint a picture mathematically that we're mostly doing the same activities all day, every day. What do you think how many days or hours during your life you're doing something that will be really remembered? Either by you or someone else. Actually, especially by you. We all know that feeling that something is a significant event, whether it is a bad or good one and whether it is small or big. And we know that we will probably remember it for the rest of our life. It is sort of stuck in our brains forever. I remember simple silly things from my childhood while I can't really remember some (or the majority) of so-called Big Events. Those silly things were such a big deal at that time that I remembered them for some reason. One could say those got written down somehow in my matrix, whatever the matrix is at this point. One such example happened during Winter Holidays while I was sitting with my family, having a completely ordinary and happy lunch. All of us together in a good mood, talking about what we normally talk about. I was around 10 years old. Then something extraordinary (for my young life) happened. One known village drunk came into our house, and he literally grabbed carrot or part of chicken from our chicken soup which was on the table in a bowl. My father reacted by grabbing him and dragging him immediately outside. I remember this event like it was yesterday for some reason. I believe this event, even though not significant at all, stuck with me for so long because it was extremely awkward, and it disturbed our peaceful lunch. I wasn't used to that, and I wasn't expecting it.

Although this may be a silly example, it is a prelude to the point I want to make. Only extremes in our lives stay written down in our brains, perhaps for life. Some of those extremes happened to us without any of our influence or activity, while others happened because we did something. Going parachuting out of the bloom would be an example of the latter one. For sure 1st time parachuting stays with us for most of our lives. Now, if we extrapolate those to our day-to-day life, both personal and business, we can notice that majority of people are constantly riding the same bicycle and the same path, sort of speak. There are a set of rules people follow, which makes them run in their own little matrix for their whole life.

Take any profession or any professional. The majority are constantly discussing topics that are solely in their domain. Most for their whole life. People they socialize with are then again in the same (or similar) domain. Not necessarily professionally but like-minded in some way. This leaves no space for extremes in the discussion, a difference of opinions or behaviors. According to settled unwritten rules of life, it is almost always expected that people choose one career and professional path and pursue it till the end. And it is not only for poor people or the middle class, as the majority of rich also behave the same way. How many musicians can you name that completely changed their music style and not just once but a couple of times? There are some, of course, but the majority didn't. The same goes for many different artists. And for sure, the same goes for people pursuing so-called standard careers. By standard careers, I mean lawyers, doctors, economists, different business professions, et cetera. Of course, it is hard to leave the profession for which you studied many years and spent an additional 20 in perfecting it. This is understood, but most people won't even try anything different just for fun. It doesn't have to be a complete change of profession. The profession can still be the main focus, but not trying anything else in whole life is something that really shouldn't happen so often in society.

As Rober Heinlein famously said in his novel Time Enough for Love:

*"A human being should be able to change a diaper, plan an invasion, butcher a hog, conn a ship, design a building, write a sonnet, balance accounts, build a wall, set a bone, comfort the dying, take orders, give orders, cooperate, act alone, solve equations, analyze a new problem, pitch manure, program a computer, cook a tasty meal, fight efficiently, die gallantly. **Specialization is for insects.**"*

I really like the last sentence – *specialization is for insects* – as it greatly paints how humans have so much more capabilities and possibilities in their life, but they mostly focus on (or specialize) only one thing. This is significant in many ways. If most people are not even trying to dive in slightly into their own possibilities and potential, whether those are physical or mental, then what kind of global society are we living in. If aliens were to spectate us for a couple of days, they would probably return back immediately to where they came from. Just think about it for a second. Looking at human society from the above (alien) perspective, it would seem we're little ants following the same path strolling in limits of our own matrixes. You go to school, you go to an additional school, then you go to work, then you have children, then you work some more, and then you die.

Throw into that equation dozens of short vacations that every human being will have during their lifetime, and you receive an average life mixture. Now don't get me wrong, some stability and structure are reasonable and necessary, but society should enable more for most people.

Therefore, let's use Maslow's hierarchy of needs as a mirror to see whether, as a society, we live in constraints and 'matrixes,' or we blossom to our highest potentials. Maslow's hierarchy of needs is a theory and framework in psychology encompassing a five-tier model of human needs, often described as hierarchical levels within a pyramid. From the bottom of the hierarchy upwards, the needs are: physiological (air, water, food, shelter, sleep, clothing, reproduction), safety (personal security, employment, resources, health), love and belonging needs (friendship, intimacy, family, sense of connection), esteem (respect, self-esteem, status, recognition, freedom), and self-actualization (desire to become the most that one can be). Needs lower down in the hierarchy must be satisfied before individuals can attend to the needs higher up. Basically, it could be described as levelling up in video games. And while many successfully level up in video games, it is not the case in real life, unfortunately. Stating that, it would be interesting to see what percentage of society is constantly levelling up and what percentage is stuck in, let's say matrix (or level) number 2 for their whole life. Here by no means, I refer to financial levelling but mostly on intellectual, spiritual, and overall explorational. While self-actualizing (Maslow Hierarchy) is a process that for most span lifetime many do not achieve it at all nor reach near to it. Self-actualization is achieved when you're able to reach your full potential. However, being genuinely self-actualized is considered the exception rather than the rule since most people are working to meet more pressing day-to-day needs. Having said that, one rather important characterization of self-actualization is getting frequent peak experiences. According to Maslow,□ a peak experience involves:

"Feelings of limitless horizons opening up to the vision, the feeling of being simultaneously more powerful and also more helpless than one ever was before, the feeling of ecstasy and wonder and awe, the loss of placement in time and space with, finally, the conviction that something extremely important and valuable had happened, so that the subject was to some extent transformed and strengthened even in his daily life by such experiences."

Is this "ecstasy" something that many people can achieve? I mean for sure, with the help of recreational drugs such as MDMA or its street name ecstasy, but I am not here talking about that kind. There aren't many analyses and papers published to see how many people are self-actualized, but one can conclude it is fairly low since most of humanity is, as we stated, grinding in their own little matrixes.

Maslow agrees with that as he states that only a small percentage of the population reaches self-actualization. The concept of achieving those higher levels offers a variety of interpretations because it differs based on each person. One individual may feel that their maximum potential is to be the manager of a local clothing store after steadily climbing the ladder following high school graduation. For this person, this achievement will provide all the happiness he or she needs, and the person will be fulfilled. Another person may feel that a position of local manager is below his or her potential, so getting the title would not be adequate for happiness. This logic goes to all levels and all positions, career-wise. Perhaps the CEO of a really big company thinks of himself as truly self-actualized, but in many cases, it is the exact opposite. Many people are simply far too under-motivated to achieve the peak of their potentials in different categories, not just in one like being CEO of a company.

So, what can be done about that? How could we enable a society where more people would be happier, achieve their true selves, and escape their little matrix. Those questions are hard and almost impossible to answer, but since society is constantly developing, it can be expected that in a hundred or more years, humankind will reach that kind of consciousness that we would create building blocks necessary for every human to reach their true potential.

Perhaps a potential solution could be to reshape society in a way where people could have many different careers throughout their life. Not that it isn't possible today, albeit only a few succeed. There are many reasons why it is so, but societal constraints and matrix models of current schooling, business, and economic establishments are the first that leap to mind. Nevertheless, I think political figures and decision-makers should spend more time thinking about how to make such a society possible. Because wandering around like NPC's (Non-Player Characters) through life for sure is not the best way for humans to spend their time on this planet. One can draw attention here to the non-equilibrium analysis stating that: without any substantial reorganization of the system, the oscillations will swing more and more wildly until such a reorganization is achieved via collapse. Perhaps collapse will, in turn, reorganize society so that every person achieves their full potential. Perhaps it will be the complete opposite, but one thing is for sure - we all need to try our best to create a society where more people are happy. Happy with themselves and their own mind.

"We have two lives, and the second begins when we realize
we only have one."
– CONFUCIUS

What would happen if a modern human was transferred 2000 years from now in history?

"The lessons of history would suggest that civilizations move in cycles. You can track that back quite far - the Babylonians, the Sumerians, followed by the Egyptians, the Romans, China. We're obviously in a very upward cycle right now, and hopefully, that remains the case. But it may not."
– ELON MUSK

Current society is progressing at a rather fast speed, and it's been like that for many years. We are constantly inventing amazing new things. New devices, new solutions to old problems, and new mathematical theorems and physical laws are discovered so quickly that it is immensely hard to follow and stay in tune. To be fair, in recent times, we're mostly developing newer versions of existing things, and not many original inventions are going on, especially in the mathematics and physics category, but still, there is a constant influx of new things in this world. Additionally, there is an even bigger influx of information received by every individual every day. Previously, in ancient times, the average person received an amount of information that is not even comparable to today's person. Perhaps we could compare today's person one hour of information with ancient people one month or more. However, how much quality is in this information? What do we really learn from the enormous amount of data and information? Well, looking at the average person – not much. It seems like our brain in modern times is just like an internet router – receiving and processing data but without any logic what to actually do with it.

In that sense, I think it would be interesting to hypothesize about placing a modern person into the time around Roman Empire or some 2000 years ago. At that time, 99% of the things we use today were not available. The modern person is using all those things (electricity, lights, heating, warm water, condoms, surgeries, automobiles, planes, and so on), and probably have some info on how those are built, but would he or she be able to invent any of them if placed, say year 20 BC? Remember that this person is coming from a faraway future (2021) where he/she went through many years of education and has all possible knowledge about everything in the palm of his hand via mobile phone. However, what is all this knowledge worth if that person cannot manage to re-invent any of the things he used in his modern world. So, in that case, let's imagine what would average Joe (35 years old) do in these historical times? Would he perhaps discover electricity or place a patent for long distant communication?

So imaginary average Joe born in 1986 is 35 years old when he somehow found a way to go to year 20BC. It's a sudden and unexplainable journey. He doesn't have any way to prepare or bring numerous books or his smartphone with him. Average Joe is dressed in linen pants and has a standard haircut which could pass completely normal for historic Christ times. Now what? He has this immense "knowledge" in his head, but what to do with it and how to share it with those ancient people. At least he could become a new Jesus with that kind of knowledge if he manages to convince different people that he is actually from the future and has so much valuable info to share with them. That is, of course, if he also manages to save himself from not being hanged or beaten down because of his modern 'voodoo' madness.

When he first arrives in, say, ancient Rome, nothing seems very strange, nor to him nor to people around him. He is aware that in Rome of that time they, of course, didn't have electricity, cars, mobile phones or anything that we're used to in our modern lives. Also, he doesn't look weird to people of that time as he looks very similar to them, if not the same. People didn't change physically in the last 2000 years. Of course, clothes and haircuts changed, but average Joe's clothes are nothing especially weird. Well, at least not for us in modern times. Since he is wearing pants, he did get several intriguing looks on the street, mostly because Romans considered pants to be barbarous garments. Only later during Roman Empire (around the 6th century), sleeved tops and trousers had become the official uniform of the Empire. Consequently, Joe is being watched strangely on the streets as he is wearing linen pants. However, he is also watching Romans on the street doing some weird things which he can't understand just yet. Namely, Romans used urine to wash some clothes. Yes, you read that right. They packed a bunch of clothes, placed them in bowls, and then soaked them with urine. Average Joe had no idea that Romans had this "interesting" way to wash clothes. Then after a couple of days, he got acquainted with many weird traditions and activities of Romans. For example, urine was not only used for washing clothes but in many cases also as a mouthwash. Then Joe also learned that purple clothing was a status symbol reserved only for emperors and senators. This is mostly because this kind of color was not easy to achieve as it was made from murex seashells. Nowadays, everyone can wear purple, even average Joe. Oh yeah, Joe also learned that Romans like to socialize in communal toilets. Those were places where in one room (without doors), there were dozens of toilet bowls. So, Romans were sitting there, chatted with their fellow "seaters," and did their thing. With only several examples, it is clear that Romans had weird day-to-day life (compared to us today), but many other activities were similar, so Joe had a chance to talk to people and drink wine in taverns. Yes, 2000 years ago, Romans had taverns and restaurants as it seems with recent archeological discoveries. Joe was very happy to see that Romans had bars where he could describe to them all cool things from the future and perhaps help them build some of those. And so, the conversation begins with Roman guy and Joe:

- "Do you know that in 2000 years you will be able to drive 300 kilometers per hour in something we call cars!?" Joe stated laughingly, showing off his knowledge.

- "Mate, for the second time, I'm telling you, you've been drinking too much wine." Annoyed, Roman squeezed through his teeth while watching a voluptuous lady across the street.

- Joe insisted. "But.. but...Cars are a real thing, and everyone has them in 2000 years."

- "Ok, you got my curiosity. So, tell me, how are cars built exactly, and how do they work so we can build them here and now?" Roman indulged his curiosity.

- Joe pinched his nose, trying to think. "Well, you know, they have four wheels made of rubber, and then the motor is running those wheels based on valves which are then again running based on gasoline and sparks."

- Roman smiled, looking distracted. "What you say mate just now? You started inventing words?"

- "No. What words? I mean, this is how the car is working." Joe replied nervously.

- "First off – what is gasoline, and what are valves." Roman insisted.

- "You know, the gasoline and the valves."

- "No, I don't'."

- "Gasoline is liquid that comes from the earth."

- "And how come we never found it?" Roman asked.

- "Because you didn't dig deep enough into the earth."

- "Why would we do that?"

- "Well, to find gasoline."

- "Ok, this conversation is not making any sense. Can you describe in detail what cars are exactly and how they are built? Or can you make one?" Roman asked tensely.

- "No, I can't do any of those things," Joe explained.

- "So, you're making things up?"

- "No, I am not. I just can't describe in so many technical details."

- "But you're using those things every day?"

- "Yes."

- "Then you must be able to describe it or perhaps even build it?"

- "Unfortunately, no"

- "Ok, what more do you have in your so-called future?"

- "Well, we can fly with airplanes!"

- "Ok, so it seems like you're completely crazy. I'll call you Lunatic Joe from now on." Roman concluded this part of the conversation.

***

And so, the dialogue between Roman and Joe continued for hours and days, but Joe couldn't really convince Roman guy about almost anything, and that is because he couldn't really explain how things are built in the modern world. Albert Einstein's analogy comes quite nicely here to describe what our Average Joe is doing: *"If you can't explain it simply, you don't understand it well enough."* Well, Joe didn't understand any matter really well to explain it so that it is believable to someone from a completely different time.

Therefore, the question comes to mind – if the whole society is set back a couple of thousand years – would we manage to come to the same result of progress as it is today, and would it be at the same pace? Perhaps society would develop completely differently depending on how much wisdom we'd have. Then perhaps we would develop much more quickly, and we would already have flying cars and Neuralink technologies in 2021. One thing is for sure; most of the society is completely oblivious about almost everything and especially about different technological progress and about how things really work. What current society is not oblivious about is - how to dance on Tik Tok and how to receive the most likes on different social networks. Where will that kind of society lead us? Time will tell (and it is discussed in a separate chapter of this book), but I am almost sure that it leads to even more oblivion (the state of being unaware or unconscious of what is happening around one) by even more people.

Is retirement a fundamental delusion of life?

"For it is in your power to retire into yourself whenever you choose."
– MARCUS AURELIUS (Meditations)

We all know the big story. You are born, you go to kindergarten, you go to school, to university, then you start your career, and then after several years or decades, you start dreaming of retirement. "Oh, if I could only retire now to have more time for myself and family" – the majority of people say during their career and lifetime. Oh, what will I do when I retire? Oh, that will be the joy. In my opinion, this delusion that retirement will bring something wonderful is one of the greatest delusions that this society brought to humankind. Just imagine the unbearable nonsense of this paradigm – you work until you're 67, and then you will receive something from your government to "enjoy" life. Which life exactly at 67? I mean, there are many people that still feel great at 67, but there are also many who die a couple of months or a couple of years after retirement. Yet, most people cannot even fathom the limited time they have left in this world. Everybody is constantly planning something like we will all live 200 years, while the truth is completely different. There's an interesting quote from Mike Tyson which could be applied here: "Everybody has a plan until they get punched in the mouth." It is so true in many life situations, and it is also true for this situation. Getting punched in the mouth here is the realization of how much time many people actually have after retirement and how much time they spent on dreadful day-to-day and year-to-year rat race of meaningless jobs and activities.

Now, this is a problem of this kind of society that we built, of course. For some to enjoy, some others need to work meaningless jobs until they drop dead. Literally and figuratively. It is what it is, but there must be a better way to organize society. By some statistics, 85% of people hate their job. I mean, this is an insane society if we look at it - the big majority of humans hate what they do for most of their life. Moreover, they are doing it in their prime years. Then they (we) retire and then die. A nice little lie, or should I say deception, that has been perpetuated throughout society for centuries. Sure, one could argue that living today is better than living at any time in history. And this is probably true. Nevertheless, whether we live the best lives today than in whole human history, we still must acknowledge that the concept of retirement as we know it today is complete and utter delusion or, should I say, error. I stated 'error' because it really is a mathematical miscalculation or error of human contribution to society via his or her 'worthy' lifespan. Can't this calculation be a little bit different so that even though some will probably still have to work in a job they hate, possibly they could opt out earlier and still live a somehow satisfying life? It is a romantic thought, but it is one that is worth considering.

But what is happening in reality? Governments are prolonging the time people have to work to receive their jolly retirement check. One explanation for that is that people are living longer. And this is true. But it is also true that today we have machines doing much of the work people did just recently. On the other hand, we also have more and more greedy people where money pours by gallons every hour, and it is still not enough for them. The biggest problem lies exactly there. If wealth could be distributed somehow differently, then perhaps billions and billions of people wouldn't have to work until they die at work.

Additional ambivalence for people is that they are constantly fed romantic falsehoods about how they will enjoy vacations and drink cocktails in the Bahamas if they work hard. Surely if you're working hard towards some goal, that is very admiring and a good baseline to achieve some kind of happiness. Nonetheless, many people are working hard only to save for a two-week vacation, after which many are disappointed. Those places from postcards never look the same, are mostly crowded, and you wander around the city pointlessly just to be able to shoot some fancy Instagram photos, which then signal to your friends and acquaintances that you're successful and happy. Traveling is great, don't get me wrong, but many people are doing it because of all erroneous reasons, and they end up unsatisfied and in debt many times. This debt (not only from vacations) prolongs then to next year, and so you start racing the famous rat race. This is only one of the things that enable retirement delusion to grow even bigger. Because you then think," I will finally travel all the time when I am in retirement." Yes, you could if you have money (which the majority don't have), but again it's not the same fun as it is in your 30's 40's or 50's.

Then there's the constant need to buy things. Better, newer, more expensive things just because you received a better paycheck (lifestyle inflation). And then you end up on the same wealth as you were at the beginning of your career with regards to actual freedom. But hey, you have all the expensive things, right? This again feeds the delusion. Oh, but one day... The goal is near, I am almost there, just this one more thing, and I will arrive at my destination. The end of a journey is near. But is life really a journey with a destination? Quote that "life is a journey" is one of the most common analogies in the world, but it is mostly wrongly interpreted. According to great British philosopher Alan Watts, it's terribly misworded and has become misused as he explains that life cannot be a journey since "It doesn't have some destination that it ought to arrive at." Richard Branson's wording in relation to Alan Watts says it well. Branson is saying how Watts explains that traditional systems of education have skewed the meaning of life (towards arriving at a destination) by placing too much importance on progressing through school and college to a career. And he also makes his point by saying that far too many people live to retire and therefore cheat themselves of an exciting existence.

Instead of seeing life as a journey, Alan believed we should experience it like a musical thing. Songs are playful, unpredictable, and have moments of brilliance all throughout the composition. *"Same with dancing, you don't aim at a particular spot in the room because that's where you should arrive. The whole point of dancing is the dance."*

Consequently, the whole point of living is to live life. Not to wait for retirement. As waiting for retirement is not really living. In Allan Watt's dance analogy, this would be like you're sitting on a table waiting for the dance to end so that you can dance then without music when everyone is gone. Oh, the world we're living in. Adding to that, do you know what percentage of people actually live to their retirement? Or how many years do people live on average after they retire? Well, statistics are not very good. By that, I mean statistics on life expectancy compared to the prolonged time for retirement.

The United Nations estimates a global average life

expectancy of 72.6 years for 2019. This is significantly more than in previous centuries. By Our World in Data analysis, a newborn baby in 1800 could expect a rather short life, no matter where in the world it was born. In the 1950s, newborns had the chance of a longer life if they were lucky enough to be born in the right place. In recent decades all regions of the world have made very substantial progress, and it was those regions that were worst-off in 1950 that achieved the biggest progress since then. The divided world of 1950 has been narrowing. Globally the life expectancy increased from less than 30 years to over 72 years in just a couple of centuries. And this progress was not achieved in a few places. In every world region, people can today expect to live much longer than in the previous century.

So far, so good. Actually great. So many people living a longer life is an astonishing result. However, on the other hand, people are expected to work longer, much longer, and thus the "freedom" time is also shrinking. Not to mention the quality of that "freedom" time. Needless to say, working by you're almost 70 and then looking forward to retirement doesn't make sense, but it greatly fits a narrative of illusion called – free, happy, and long golden years. Then how to distant yourself from this grand illusion of retirement? There is a simple equation – spend less than you earn and, in return, try to achieve financial freedom in some reasonable timespan. That is, of course, if you want to. There are still (fortunately) many people who like their jobs, and they should enjoy them. Nevertheless, I think both groups (people who like their job and people who don't) should consider finding ways to stop living in a world of grand retirement delusion. Not everybody can become a monk. But there are other ways. As Naval Ravikant, Indian-American entrepreneur, investor, and thinker stated:

*"Essentially, what you want to get everybody is retirement. But not the - I'm 65 years old, sitting in a nursing home, collecting a check' retirement. **Retirement is when you stop sacrificing today for some imaginary tomorrow.** When today is complete, in and of itself, you're retired."*

After this quote, one may wonder – well, why am I naming this chapter as "Retirement the great delusion" while also stating and quoting that goal should be so that everyone is retired. That's kind of an oxymoron, but if we follow Naval's excellent analogy of scarifying today for some imaginary tomorrow, then we get the whole picture. This is, of course, easier said than done, but by little steps, humanity should walk towards a future where the present moment is not immolated by great delusion.

Expensive vacations are not the solution, expensive cars are not solutions, and escaping into constant work is also not the solution. This is only prolonging the inevitable. I mean, "You can cut all the flowers, but you cannot keep Spring from coming." At least not with the same set of tools and mindset. Tools consisting of schooling and a journey through life to reach the final destination need to fundamentally change if we want to distance ourselves from grand illusion. Some would propose that perhaps Universal Basic Income (UBI) is the solution. But I would argue that this is far from the solution. It could even be a bigger issue. Humans are competitive artistic beings, and UBI would probably only make people duller and more lethargic with no desire to do anything. Some set of rewards for great work needs to be in society. We cannot all sit on our asses, watching Netflix all day while receiving 1000$ from our governments. This could actually look like early and depressing retirement for many people. Even though the current political and economic system is playing with some kind of rudimentary UBI during the COVID crisis, I believe this is not the solution for the future. People need to accept automatization and robotization with joy and not with fear. Because if we implement a reorganization of society in such a way where robots and AI take the majority of our (current) jobs, that should only mean that humans have more time for their creative, artistic jobs, which are high on Maslow's Hierarchy of needs. At the end of the day, human beings are not meant to do repetitive, dull work all day throughout their lives. We are much more, and society should someday really enable all people to reach their potential, whatever that may be for any individual walking on this Earth. For some, it may be painting, for some writing songs, for some inventing new things, but probably nobody would choose to flip burgers. Robots will do that very soon, and when their parts deteriorate, they should be sent to retirement (or metal garbage in this case), and humans should pursue their desires without fear of failed grand delusion.

One day, will the whole world speak English or Chinese?

"But if thought corrupts language, language can also corrupt thought."
– GEORGE ORWELL, 1984

This question came to my mind because I live in a predominantly Western World where most news, media, and information align with what the United States is doing (and saying). Almost all movies on television are from Hollywood, and major news channels are broadcasting similar things as you can see on CNN and

NBC. Virtually all music is recorded in English, even though the singer does not speak native English. Now you may ask – ok, but what does that have to do with the topic of this chapter. Well, there won't be any impact for everyone who is currently born, but if we think about the not-so-distant future (say 500 years), things could get "complicated." Note that this hypothesis or argument can also be made about the Chinese language. Nonetheless, let's dive into more details as the "final" language is not important; the important part is the argument that perhaps in the future, one language will prevail.

First, we need to note that data concerning the number of people who speak English in the world is somehow unreliable. However, even with the ballpark number, we can see the trend. One trend is related to the number of native speakers, and one is associated with the overall number of people who can speak English and understand it, but it's not their native/primary language. In the world, it is estimated that there are around 360 million native English speakers. Countries with a majority of native English speakers are as follows: Antigua and Barbuda, Australia, the Bahamas, Barbados, Belize, Canada, Dominica, Grenada, Guyana, Ireland,

Jamaica, New Zealand, Saint Kitts and Nevis, Saint Lucia, Saint Vincent, the Grenadines, Trinidad and Tobago, United Kingdom, and the United States of America.

On the other hand, the list of countries where English is an official language (or one of the official languages) is much longer: Botswana, Cameroon, Fiji, Ghana, India, Kenya, Kiribati, Liberia, Malta, the Marshall Islands, Mauritius, Namibia, Nigeria, Pakistan, Palau, Papua New Guinea, the Philippines, Rwanda, Samoa, Seychelles, Sierra Leone, Singapore, the Solomon Islands, Sri Lanka, Sudan, South Africa, South Sudan, Swaziland, Tanzania, Uganda, Zambia, and Zimbabwe. Now that's a pretty significant number of countries. Yet in how many countries do people speak and understand English really well, and how many people in the whole world can speak English? There are different calculations. However, most statisticians agree that around 2 billion or more than 1/4 of world inhabitants speak English. That makes English the most prominent language by the number of speakers. Good enough, but one would say this is far away from the overall world population of 7,5 billion. And indeed, it is very far. However, in just a couple of hundred years, many things could change.

For sure, English currently appears to be in an unassailable position in the modern world to become a global language where most of the world population will speak some form of it. In the Middle Ages, Latin seemed to be set as the language of education and culture, as did French in the 18th Century. But circumstances change, and several factors might precipitate such a change once again but this time in favor of English winning not just the battle but the whole war. I already mentioned some of these circumstances: Hollywood, movies, music, news, propaganda, et cetera.

So, let's imagine that the current trend and English/Western propaganda continues for additional 200 or 300 years. Everybody will probably have devices (potentially implanted) that will translate languages instantly. Those devices are available already, but they are not yet widespread. The majority of games, television, and music will be in English. Babies will be born and bombarded by the English language (as they are currently by bizarre cartoons). Now imagine that politicians worldwide agree that one government is the only solution to current problems. Then that one-world government needs to speak the same language. The first choice would then probably be English. Sidenote: *with recent coronavirus pandemic development, the frontrunner could easily become the Chinese language.*

Many countries and languages would for sure fight against the official usage of English for years and years. But as more and more schools open where English is the official language, more people and more governments would decide that the simplest way to continue living is to use the English language as a baseline.

If that happens to 80% of the population (or even 60%), then the war is over – the English language has won. Looking at an even more distant future, say 1000 years, probably no one will even remember any other languages. Maybe even English will not exist then, as some kind of machine language will prevail. Potentially with technologies like Musk's Neuralink, we will not even speak since we will possibly have the capability to read each other's minds in one way or another. Not my words; Elon Musk indicated that in one conversation. And it's not that this is not happening already in one way or another. Remember when people talked in person for hours or even on the telephone. Now, this is mostly gone. Everybody is typing on their mobile phones, even when they are sitting together in a bar. The language used in those typing sessions is becoming more and more poorly written, with the combination of thousands of silly memes and words. Continuation of this trend could very well lead to a universal language in hundreds or thousands of years. Many languages are now forgotten, and perhaps many more will be. Young people in the year 2500 will probably learn in their history books about some archaic languages such as Croatian, Norwegian, or Choctaw. Ok, the latter one, traditionally spoken by the Native American Choctaw people of the southeastern United States, is already mostly forgotten. But that only adds to the point I'm trying to make. One thing is certain; the language map will undoubtedly change. And with current globalization trends, this will be in favor of one or two languages.

What would happen without electricity for a year?

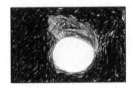

"The day when we shall know exactly what electricity is will chronicle an event probably greater, more important than any other recorded in the history of the human race. The time will come when the comfort, the very existence, perhaps, of man will depend upon that wonderful agent."
– NIKOLA TESLA

The world without electricity today is unimaginable. We depend on electricity for almost everything in our daily lives. Lights in our homes and cities first come to mind. But the power of electricity is so widespread that probably there isn't any field of humanity where it doesn't play one of the main roles. Yet, we humans lived without its application and widespread use for 99,99% of our time on this planet.

Electricity wasn't invented per se, it was present from the beginning of times, but we didn't know how to harvest it for our usage. People first started noticing something electric when they became aware of shocks from electric fish. In ancient Egypt, they were referring to these fish as the "Thunderer of the Nile." At that time, as far as we know, they didn't have the slightest idea what electricity really was. Ancient Greek, Roman, and Arabic physicians also reported about those electric fish. Some ancient writers witnessed about numbing effect of electric shocks caused by catfish. However, what is very important, they knew that those shocks could travel along conducting objects.

Then around the ancient Mediterranean, people knew that certain objects such as rods of amber could be rubbed, for example, with cat's fur to attract light objects such as feathers. Ancient people around 500 BCE also knew something about static electricity, but they didn't quite know what to do with that. Researchers and archeologists also discovered different pots with copper inside, and they believed that those were used as batteries in ancient Roman sites. Perhaps they used those batteries for lightning, but we don't really know.

Fast forward many years ahead, we discovered and applied electricity, but there are still many misconceptions about who really "discovered" it. Some give credit to Benjamin Franklin for discovering electricity. However, his experiments only helped establish the connection between lightning and electricity and nothing more.

Some 50 years after Benjamin Franklin's experiment, Italian physicist Alessandro Volta discovered that particular chemical reactions could produce electricity, and based on that, in 1800, he constructed an early electric battery that produced a stable electric current. Thus, he could be accredited as the first person to create a steady flow of electrical charge. Additionally, Volta created the first transmission of electricity by linking positively-charged and negatively-charged connectors and driving an electrical charge through them. A curious fella' that Alessandro, for sure.

Then we have Michael Faraday as he created electric dynamo in 1931. This basically solved the problem of generating electricity in a constant and practical way. This invention consequently opened the door to Thomas Edison for his invention of the light bulb in 1878. He wasn't the only one, as British scientist Joseph Swan invented the same around those years. Electric illumination was groundbreaking because previously, all lightning was based on gas and oil burning inside the glass. I mean, some form of light bulbs had been invented by others, but theirs was the first practical one as it could emit light for hours on end. Swan and Edison later created a joint company where they produced the first practical filament lamp. Edison followed that by illuminating New York streets with electric lamps in September 1882.

Later in the 1800's and early 1900s, Serbo-Croatian engineer, inventor, and all-around electrical wizard Nikola Tesla became a crucial contributor to the birth of commercial electricity. He had so many inventions that it's hard to name them all. He was one of the most prolific and innovative engineers and inventors of the nineteenth and twentieth centuries. It is believed that Nikola Tesla held somewhere in the order of 196 patents for his tech across 26 countries worldwide. He also worked with Edison, and it is well known that they had many disputes regarding the usage of AC vs. DC.

Luckily Tesla managed to convince American society that the future of electricity is with AC rather than DC. With his inventions, he is probably the biggest contributor to the world of electricity as we know it today. Of course, there were also others who worked to bring the use of electricity to where it is today, including Scottish inventor James Watt, Andre Ampere, a French mathematician, and German mathematician and physicist George Ohm. And so, it was obviously not just one person who discovered electricity. While the concept of electricity was known for hundreds and perhaps thousands of years, when the time came to develop it commercially and scientifically, dozens of great minds worked on the problem simultaneously and through many years.

So undoubtedly, many coincidences, genius people, and a lot of curiosity led to finding out what electricity really is and how to harvest it for our use. Electricity can be almost singlehandedly awarded as one of the biggest factors to all our technological and societal development. Without electricity, we can for sure agree we wouldn't have information and communication technologies which are today's main wheels of progress and development. Yet, we could also argue that electricity is then to be blamed for increasingly more *"broken wheels"* that we're witnessing in our society caused by such progress.

In modern times we can notice that many people are blaming technological development for the biggest problems in society. However, if we're to be very blunt and concise, this technological development all started only because of electricity. So, we could easily blame electricity for all those changes. Without electricity, we wouldn't have smartphones or social networks, which are changing today's society completely. Yet, without electricity, we also wouldn't have food or water distribution as we are used to in our lives. Or any other commodity for that matter.

Electricity (among other things) enabled humans to produce food and other products on a large scale. This led to a big surplus of food and other products, which again led to people reproducing more than ever and dying less. In the 1800s, there were less than 1 billion people on Earth, and now there are 7,800,000 000 people on Earth. Just imagine the growth in only 200 years. So obviously, this growth was made possible because of electricity (and some other factors, of course), but this growth also made possible that the stupidity of large masses grows similarly. Introduction from movie Idiocracy comes to my mind when I think about it:

"As the 21st century began, human evolution was at a turning point. Natural selection, the process by which the strongest, the smartest, the fastest, reproduced in greater numbers than the rest, a process which had once favored the noblest traits of man, now began to favor different traits. Most science fiction of the day predicted a future that was more civilized and more intelligent. But as time went on, things seemed to be heading in the opposite direction. A dumbing down. How did this happen? Evolution does not necessarily reward intelligence. With no natural predators to thin the herd, it began to simply reward those who reproduced the most, and left the intelligent to become an endangered species."

Idiocracy analogy is nice, but what does all that have to do with a potential electricity blackout scenario? Well, today, every possible scientific discovery is available for us and for our day-to-day use, but if some of those suddenly disappear, we are likely helpless. Not only that, but our long-time habits such as usage of electricity hinders our lives completely in case of a blackout, and especially in modern society. Several days is not a problem for most, but then after weeks, problems start to be so large that it seems like a collapse of society.

In the modern world, we didn't have many prolonged blackouts, but if it were to happen, say for a year, well, then we're in big trouble. So, let's examine how the potential timeline of blackout would impact society day by day. Before that, I need to mention also real-life cases of blackout in modern society. For example, hospital patients in Venezuela found out in 2019 during a five-day nationwide blackout that power cuts can do much more than just turn out the lights. Doctors and staff were helpless. In almost total darkness, they watched patients dying in front of them. Without electricity the lifts could not work and what is more important many life assisting machines could not work. Consequently, 26 people died. Some because they couldn't get vital dialysis and other treatments, and some because surgeons could not operate in darkness. Terrifying situation indeed.

Then we have a very recent example being played out in Texas, USA, in February 2021. The crisis was the result of two harsh winter storms sweeping across the United States on February 10–11 and 13–17. More than

4.5 million homes and businesses in Texas were left without electricity, some for several days. By February 19, at least 32 people died, with deaths linked to carbon monoxide poisoning, drownings, house fires, car crashes, and hypothermia. By February 21, the death toll had increased to 70. Not so many deaths, one could presume, considering the number of people in Texas. However, have in mind this lasted only for two weeks. There are also several cases around the world throughout history, but none lasting for a really long time. Each prolonged day would bring additional deaths and huge problems for society. So, let's try to hypothesize on that prolonged imaginary scenario and perhaps, in this case, for the whole world.

On the first day, people would be very surprised, especially if they hear somehow that it is happening worldwide. That information would set a spark for anxiety and fear. Nevertheless, one day without electricity is not a huge problem since most essential institutions and facilities have backup generators from which they can produce electricity. Most citizen buildings, however, would be in complete darkness. That means problems for older citizens as elevators are not working. Also, today's society mostly can't think of what to do in the evening without television or the internet. A huge problem for the boredom of people but not really an essential problem for the world. Perhaps one day of blackout would be even good for many people since then they would be forced to talk to their spouses and other family members.

The second day starts, and electricity is nowhere to be seen. Still, the whole world is in the dark. Well, at least that part where there is no sunlight at that particular time. Nevertheless, darkness is not such a big problem. Many other things are, such as heating, water supply, gas supply, and so forth. Without electricity, gas stations cannot pump gas unless they have a generator or an alternate source of power. Some stations have generators to work 24 hours, some perhaps 48, but inevitably if the power outage continues, this becomes a huge problem for overall transport. Let's say that on day two, most gas pumps do not work properly, then immediately we have problems with transporting essential things such as food. So, the food chain could become broken very soon, and this is the real problem. Most of today's communities cannot live long before running out of food in their homes, as rare people live self-sustainable lives. People are going a couple of times per week to stores to buy groceries. To be fair, some of those are not essential, but as fridges are getting empty, so the concern levels grow in each household. Add to that reminder that electricity is still gone in the whole world. For a second day. Anxiety and fear triples. But there is hope for day three.

Day three arises. Still nothing. The whole world is still in electricity blackout. But now, many essential services will run out of backup electrical power. Depending on the country's policies, in rare places can hospitals work normally. And when hospitals run out of electricity, dire problems start to arise, as explained in Venezuela example. Elevators necessary to transport patients are not in service anymore. But that's the least of worry for hospitals. So many devices in hospitals responsible for keeping people alive are near to their dead-end — literally both for devices and patients. Also, without lights, obviously, you can not operate properly on people. Basically, if the hospital is out of electricity and backup power, they are doomed completely. So, if hospitals are in panic, people outside hospitals are also in a panic. Not that people just stopped getting injured or sick all of a sudden. But what to do with them now? You can not bring them to the hospital that is not working. So, more panic among the people. In the majority of households, the discussion is solely around what is happening in the world. Everyone is in panic, and there is no word from your favorite politician. How could it be? I mean, you can not turn on your television or internet portal. Food in the refrigerator is also running out, and the nearby store is either not working, or most food is missing. What about tap water? Well in majority households water comes out of the pipe which is connected to city water. And those get filtered powered by electricity. So, if you even can get some water, this water isn't drinkable. Then you need to heat it up to boiling water so that it becomes drinkable. But where to heat it. On gas oven, of course, but for how long. How long could this last?

Fast forward to two weeks without electricity. Now it is whole mayhem in the world. Everything is collapsing. All the things that people are used to, like television, the internet, social networks, and many other (really not important) things, are in a blackout. But those are just the small things even though they seem like the most important things ever in their daily lives for the modern human. But hey, without cute internet kitties, one can live normally. Nonetheless, the internet is not only for those things. Without the internet, nothing works. And I mean almost literally nothing in today's society. Try to shop in the store without internet (if the store works because of blackout), try to go to ATM, try to call anyone. Without global electricity, no modern phone will work. You are in a panic, and you cannot call your mother on the other end of the country or continent. What about food? Well, if you live in a village and have your own farm perhaps you can do something. But if you have a big farm, well, that one also isn't working without electricity, so the livestock starts dying. If you have two pigs and a couple of cows, you're probably good for a year or more in this situation. But bigger farms are doomed as those animals are being fed with the help of electricity or, being more precise - with machines that run on electricity. Consequently, this then adds to the problem of breaking the food chain completely.

Fast forward two more weeks – now one month without electricity. People are panicking more than ever. Additionally, they now really don't have any more topics to talk about with their spouses. Not that this is not an essential problem, but it aids to anxiety because only topics on the table are; what is happening, will we survive, where to get food, is this all being done on purpose, are the riches of the world hiding somewhere waiting for all of us to go extinct? The latter is a rather interesting question. In this situation of horror, what would happen with billionaires and those in power? Of course, they would handle the situation much better because they have all possible resources in their hands.

And additionally, many also prepared beforehand. Not that I am predicting this will happen, but did you know how many articles appeared in the last two years named something like this:

"Billionaire bunkers: How the 1% are preparing for the apocalypse."

Hundreds, probably thousands, and I am not exaggerating at all. One specific article about bunkers continues by describing how many of the world's elite, including hedge fund managers, sports stars, and tech executives, have chosen to design their own secret shelters to house their families. Gary Lynch, general manager of Texas-based Rising S Company (steel bunker producer), says 2016 sales for their custom top-notch underground bunkers grew 700% compared to 2015. Now, this is something to think about. With regards to electricity, those bunkers mostly have an underground power generator, and they have a stockpile of fuel to keep the generator running for a long time. This then, of course, leads to the conclusion that elites of the world would be covered in a situation of a total electricity blackout. Well, at least more than the average Joe.

Needless to say, I am not here stating that anyone is foreseeing that this kind of apocalypse could or will happen, but the matter of the fact is that riches of the world are more prepared, and they are buying bunkers like crazy in the last decade.

So, in our imaginary scenario, last month, some 0.001% of people perhaps moved to bunkers and are observing what is happening with the world, but they also are not secured as no one knows when will electricity get back. Bunkers can sustain life perhaps for a year, two, or five but not indefinitely. Nevertheless, their anxiety levels are much lower than those of average people living in 50 square meter apartments where their main topic is now – "what the fuck is happening and should I maybe start to think about suffocating my neighbor when shit hits the fan because he/she is very loud and potentially good source of food."

And so, shit did hit the fan 100%. Weeks turned into months, and no light at the end of the tunnel. Now six months into the blackout and society is on the verge of complete collapse. Famine is now widespread as food chains are entirely collapsed. No food can be seen in stores; actually, there are no open stores to be found. Some self-sustainable people are coping quite well, but their family estates are being taken over and robbed by so many hungry and possibly quite unstable and dangerous people. Normal people transformed into something unrecognizable, perhaps best described as some characters from the movie Mad Max. Roads around the world are collapsed almost completely since people just left their cars on the streets in lack of gas and electricity for Teslas of the world. Basically, everything is collapsing like a house of cards. Sole fabrics of society are broken into pieces, and it seems like no one can sew them back together. And the most important thing that is being broken is the human mind. Rare people can cope with this kind of situation - suicide and crime are on the highest levels in history. And did I also mention that without electricity, prison doors are opened very soon? Probably in the first month. So then, triple murderer and rapist Joe with his three friends arrive at your door asking where your wife is. Not an easy challenge to resolve now, is it?

In the meantime, experts are trying to resolve the electricity problem, but nothing works. Every passing day it is becoming almost clear that there is no hope. We once knew how to set up electricity for the whole world, and while this knowledge is still here, collapsed society is disabling any progress to be made. In a world of chaos, it is hard to re-establish something that was a basic necessity for human survival. Well, at least in the last 100 years.

On the other hand, most animals and plants in the wild are thriving. However, those animals that are in possession of humans - not so much. According to the Food and Agriculture Organization (FAO), the world has 1.468 billion head of cattle. That's a lot, and those animals cannot survive without electricity while being captivated by humans. Blackouts disarmed people with the ability to feed them, so they mostly died. That's a lot of cattle to die in such a short period. Corpses of cattle (and humans) around the world contribute to the development of different diseases, which only speeds up society's complete collapse. Can this be an extinction event for humanity or at least for 90 something percent of humanity? Perhaps, because so many of us are used to modern ways of living without essential things that enable this life, we are doomed very quickly. After chaos settles down and billions die, potentially the situation resolves by some magnificent new invention. Maybe Tesla's wireless electricity will see the light of the day this time around. Who knows? Hopefully, we'll never have to find out in such an awful scenario.

How come we have surnames, and what will happen with them in the future?

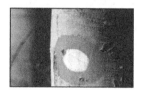

"God's last name is not Dammit."
– UNKNOWN

We all have surnames or last names. To be more precise, the majority of humans that are currently alive have surnames. Last names or surnames are so immersed in today's society that people rarely ask themselves how we got them or who was the first in the line of our ancestors to have this exact last name. For me, this is a rather interesting question for which most of us can't find the right answers. What do I mean by that? Well, for the majority of the population, it is almost impossible to find out relevant information about their ancestors past the 200 years barrier. If that much. Mostly we have some info about our great-grandparents (the parent of a person's grandparent) but not much more. Information about our great-great-great-grandparents is mostly unknown to the majority of people. We don't even know if they had the same or similar last names. Perhaps, during the course of 200 years, their (our) surname molded into something different, as is the case in numerous examples throughout history.

Those with info about their last names for 500 or more years are mostly aristocratic families (noble houses or kingship groups). Ordinary people can gather some info about their ancestors via different church books, but this is also relatively obscure. I spent a good amount of time trying to find out, but as mentioned, below 200 years barrier, it's almost impossible to find anything relevant. So obviously this is a rather interesting and important topic. But going even further, curiosity leads us to the following question. How did the first people (in history) get their surnames? This topic is something that is fascinating to dive into deeper. Hence, let's see if we have any ancient relics that will give us more data about the first person with surname and reasons for that exact surname.

It needs to be mentioned here that the concept of the last name (or family name) is a fairly recent historical development, evolving from a medieval naming practice called a 'byname.' The hunt for the oldest surname in the world is a rather challenging task, and it can take us to many different corners around the globe. Nevertheless, most of those corners lead us to several last names (or their variations) such as – COHEN, HATT, KATZ, KING, O'BRIEN, PRIEST, or SMITH. Looking at the writings of many different researchers, Biblical figures, the Teutonic Name system, and many others, it seems like there is no agreement on the original surname. Some say it's Smith, some Cohen, and some mention completely different ideas on first potential surnames. Some would then think that perhaps Christ could be a good contender for the initial surname. But one must then know that Christ is actually not the last name but a title. Christ is the English form of the Greek word, which means "Anointed One." Messiah is the English form of the same word in Hebrew. The term is a clear reference to the way that kings were chosen. So obviously, we can't find out what the first surname was and even when it happened. But perhaps even more interesting is how numerous surnames developed during thousands of years.

As mentioned previously, most of us don't even know how our surname was created, who created it and did it change from the beginning. Clearly, someone from my family tree (or anyone's) was the first one in the family to have this last name or some synonym of that last name. But what was the process of creating it? This is the interesting part for me.

Apparently, China was one of the first nations to use surnames. Then also, probably in Middle Ages, last names came to Europe. So, since I was born in Europe, there must be some relation of myself to the first human with the first surname in Europe. Well, not so fast. It is not that simple. Obviously, in Middle Ages, we didn't have only one person living in the whole of Europe. There were many. To be more precise, there were around 61 million people living in Europe during the year 1100. Out of those millions of people who got their surnames first? No one knows. But what we do know is the naming logic to some extent.

As mentioned, in Europe, last names can be traced to the Middle Ages. At that time, people lived in small villages and mostly didn't have contact with other villages. This is largely because other villages were far away. So, people from one village didn't communicate or meet with people from other villages. Villages were like a community of people where everyone knew everyone in that specific village but not much outside of that village. Hence, no need for last names.

However, this changed as villages grew and people started traveling to other villages for trade or any other activity. So, for example, Joe from Village 1 traveled to Village 2, and there he met another Joe. Well, that scenario created a problem. If Joe wanted to trade with other Joe, how would they distinguish themselves in different trade records or in spoken communication? And so, the invention of surnames seemed like a great way of distinguishing one person from another.

But how did they create those surnames – based on what? Well, mostly based on place of birth, occupation, father's name or nickname. Thus, we have the four most notable ways of surname creations: toponymic (topographic), occupational, patronymic and nickname-based. For example, a person named Joe that is coming from Boston would then be named Joe Boston. Occupational names are perhaps most known, and we have them in every country. Smith perhaps comes to mind first. Derived from the Anglo-Saxon smitan, meaning "to smite or strike," Smith is an occupational name for a person who works with metal (smith or blacksmith), probably one of the earliest jobs for which specialist skills were required.

During hundreds of years, some surnames grew while some not so much. Obviously, in bigger nations, there were more last names with huge prevalence. Based on that, in today's global world, all those last names started to mix, and one could conclude that last names with big occurrence or incidence will somehow prevail in the long run, and last names with small occurrences will perhaps go extinct in a couple of thousands of years. Could this lead to the extinction of many last names? Perhaps. For example – did you know that about 200 surnames disappeared from England and Wales in the last 100 years. Today, more surnames are lost than new ones created. Before, we had new surnames created based on someone's job or location. This is obviously not the case anymore. When did you last time hear about the creation of a new last name? Probably never. This leads us to other examples around the world which are fueling surname extinction theory.

If we look at ancient China, they had around 12000 surnames and now only around 4000. That's a big reduction especially comparing it to amount of people in today's China. And out of those, some are much more spread out than others. For example, the family names of Li, Wang, and Zhang represent around 8 percent of the overall population. A report in 2019 gives the most common Chinese surnames as Wang and Li, each shared by over 100 million people in China, with Zhang, Liu, Chen, Yang, Huang, Zhao, Wu, and Zhou making up the rest of the ten most common Chinese names.

Mathematically, in this case, the entire population can by some models converge into one or several surnames in the whole world. That's in thousands of years. Or perhaps in 200 hundred generations. This is an interesting hypothesis, and it has a basis in some mathematical models. For example, you can find out the likelihood of your surname disappearing on sites such as Forebears.io. For example, surname Smith has a global incidence of around 4,5 million (circa population of my country Croatia). On the other hand, my surname (Pernar) has a global incidence of 920 people. Therefore, it can be easily predicted that my last name will disappear in perhaps ten generations. That again raises an interesting question: Why are there so many Smiths (or any other popular last name), and will those surnames prevail globally in the next 100 000 years so that we'll perhaps have only 100 last names overall? Who knows, but it is an interesting hypothesis that does have a lot of grounds in basic mathematics. For example, let's imagine an isolated world where we only have the above-mentioned number of Smiths and the number of people carrying my last name - Pernar. Let's also imagine that half of those are females and half males. In most cases, the female takes over their last name from a male. All Smith's marrying all Pernar's, and the amount of Smith's easily grows generation by generation. So, in this case, the "battle" is basically being run between the group of 4,5 million people and 920 people. Figuratively speaking, this battle would be over before you could even calculate the odds of winning vs. losing. This little example is perhaps silly, but it does paint an interesting picture of the evolution of surnames in the not-so-distant future. Perhaps we will not even have surnames in, say, 1000 years. Maybe we'll be given surnames in a completely different way. Perhaps last names, and first names, for that matter, will mold into something similar to today's IP addresses. Who knows, but surely this world of surnames is an interesting one, and I hope one day we'll have clear and concrete evidence of the first official surname and perhaps its detailed evolution.

So, if we evolved from great apes, what would evolve from us? If anything?

"Evolution could so easily be disproved if just a single fossil turned up in the wrong date order. Evolution has passed this test with flying colours."
– RICHARD DAWKINS

People often like to say how we evolved from monkeys and that monkeys are our great ancestors. Per evolution theory, this is not exactly right, while it has some contextual sense. Namely, different species do not just evolve into other species since the process is much more complicated than that. Basically, to say that people

177

evolved from monkeys is like saying that birds evolved from fish. At the same time, it's ok saying that in a non-formal and non-scientific way, it's not how evolution actually works. More specifically, it does not work in such a horizontal way. Besides that, evolution also does not work in a way that always results in the formation of a new species.

What really runs evolution are population dynamics, genetic diversity, and genetic mutations. Of the three, to those untrained in the genetic sciences and fueled by the sensational ideas of popular science fiction, the mutation has tended to surpass the other two, which are the real driving forces without which evolution could not happen. While macro-mutations such as three-headed animals (tricephalic) do occur, this is not what evolutionary scientists think of as mutation; what they are really referring to are the spontaneous single-gene mutations that throw up an unusual characteristic that may offer a fractional survival advantage or disadvantage. At least, this is how much we know with current science. Perhaps we'll think about it in a different way in hundred years.

Nevertheless, for now, mutations are really just an influence; because populations tend not to breed far outside their immediate environment, mutations help to restore genetic diversity to what otherwise might become an overly homogeneous genetic pool. So, to demystify the question at the beginning of this chapter without delving into deep phrases of evolution theory, we could conclude that humans developed over many millions of years from early ancestors that were **like** apes. That is, humans did NOT evolve directly from apes. Instead, humans and apes both developed from the same anthropoidal (apelike) ancestor. The ancestors of humans became separate from the ancestors of apes somewhere around 8 million and 5 million years ago. After that, each group developed completely on its own. Nevertheless, modern humans and apes are still closely related. In fact, most scientists believe that humans and great apes (bonobos, gorillas, orangutans, and chimpanzees) belong to the same scientific family unit. Still, there are many significant differences between humans and apes, as we all know.

For this reason, scientists have divided the family into smaller groups. Chimpanzees, gorillas, and bonobos belong to a group called the Gorillini tribe. Orangutans belong to a group called Ponginae. Humans, on the other hand, belong to the Hominini tribe. The term hominin refers to humans and all their ancestors from the time they began developing separately from those of apes.

Also, it must be mentioned that Hominini includes the extant genera Homo and Pan but excludes the genus Gorilla.

Now, this is all fun and dandy (perhaps), but does it give us a clue as to where we could potentially evolve many years in the future? Well, not really. But it leaves us with curiosity, speculation, and imagination which is exactly the idea of this book. Looking at the problem from an uneducated high-level view, one would think that because evolution has constantly been happening for millions of years, then probably, we are evolving into something. While this can perhaps be true, it is much more complicated. Humans made it more complicated since we are so widespread in the world, which means that evolution did us good and that no additional genetic mutations are needed for us to thrive on this planet. We are thriving so well that other species are starting to suffer, and because of their suffering, potentially, we will soon also be on the verge of extinction. There have been numerous mass extinction events in the past billions of years that eliminated a significant majority of species. Some died directly because of catastrophic events, and some because their evolution and their mutations were not aligned with the present world. A good example is the panda population, as their number is constantly decreasing. One of the main reasons that the panda population has declined is environmental devastation. As the human population in China continually grows, the panda's habitat gets taken over, forcing pandas to live in smaller and, in most cases, less livable areas. Habitat destruction also leads to food shortages for pandas. However, there is also the evolutionary reason. Pandas subsist almost entirely on bamboo. Bamboo contains very little nutritional value, so pandas must eat 12-40kg every day to meet their energy needs. So, their evolutionary development led them to eat only very specific foods, and if there are shortages of those, well, then they are not in a good place. Imagine what would happen with people if we evolved in such a way that we cannot digest anything but carrots? For sure, we wouldn't be here in this world anymore, or the whole world would be filled with carrots. But we are here, and we are wondering what will happen with us in millions or billions of years.

Thinking about this topic, I came across weird ideas driven by popular science and movies but let's try to delve a little bit deeper than Terminator (or any kind of robots) even though this is not something to disregard completely as we simply don't have a clue.

Let's start from the first level, and those are different

races of human species today in the world. Looking at the very distant future, could we potentially expect that races will merge into one? This is perhaps an uneducated question but let's go with it. Today all races are mixing on a daily basis everywhere, and this is great as it wasn't the case before. Previously different races of people mainly lived in their area of land and didn't have the physical possibility to mix with other races. They would need to walk onto other continents or areas of land where other races of humans lived. Then this slowly started to happen, but still, because of some kind of idiotic and completely nonsensical racism, this didn't happen so often during most of human history. Only in relatively modern history, mixed races couples have become something normal, but there are still places in both developed and an undeveloped world where this is still not tolerated. Nevertheless, mostly it is, and it will be even more with every passing year. So, in perhaps 100 000 years or perhaps 10 million, there will be one race of people. This is, of course, a long shot, and no scientist would approve of this theory, but we really have no way of knowing what will happen with us in, say, 10 million years. Remember, Homo sapiens is only on Earth for around 300 000 years. I mean, at least, that is what we think or know based on the latest fossil evidence.

Everything can change in the course of Homo sapiens history based on one new piece of fossil evidence that we stumble upon. Nevertheless, let's continue to indulge the hypothesis of singular race.

So, if there will be one race of people, which one would it be? Probably a mix of all. However, one could also assume that there will be fewer blonde people because of a recessive blonde gene. While this at first seems like a good hypothesis, it has already been proposed and debunked by scientists. Namely, claims that blond hair will disappear have been made since 1865. Those claims can be grouped under the disappearing blonde gene phenomenon. BBC reported in 2002 that unnamed German experts concluded that blond hair would basically disappear within the span of 200 years since blond hair genes are recessive. Everybody knows that children of parents with black and blonde hair will probably not have blonde hair except if a neighbor intervenes. This is because black and brown hair are dominant alleles. Anyhow scientific community disregarded this story mentioning that it was based on a misinterpretation of recessiveness in genetics. Based on current science, gene frequency is stable unless there is selection for or against them, which does not appear to be the case for blonde hair. In large populations, even exceptionally rare genes will persevere at stable levels over extended periods of time. It also doesn't matter whether a gene is recessive or dominant. Genes fade if the population is very small (drift) or if they confer a disadvantage (selection). While blonde hair does not confer a disadvantage, no scientist can know what will happen in millions of years. So, to conclude this first point – potentially, we will have one race of people. Perhaps then we'll end racism once and for all. So far, so good. But this isn't evolution per se because we would still be the Homo sapiens, at least assuming this long shot hypothesis. So, moving on to other and weirder ideas on where could we potentially "evolve" in the distant (or even near) future.

The technological advancement that humans are constantly making is certainly influencing what and who we'll become. We are continually building new things, more things, better things, and it seems like this is the sole purpose of humanity these days especially. Well, perhaps it is. Perhaps with all those micro advancements over thousands of years, we are unknowingly building Human 2.0. In one of Joe Rogan's podcasts, he was ranting about AI and human progress, and something he said aligns perfectly with the analogy I am trying to make here. Namely, perhaps within the context of the evolution of life on Earth, humanity is playing the role of some kind of caterpillar who is about to give birth to the butterfly that is - Artificial Intelligence (AI). Our desire for the rapid and constant progression of technologies is serving a Darwinian function of survival, one that will lead to a breaking-off point between biological and synthetic life forms. When you really think about it, seems like this is exactly what we're doing as humanity on this planet. With constant progress, unavoidably, we will build something that isn't quite human, but in some ways, it still is. We don't know now whether this will be some sort of AI connected with our brains or synthetic expansion of our body, but there are clues everywhere. Elon Musk's Neuralink is hard to avoid here as they are developing implantable brain-machine interfaces. Elon Musk once said that with the implementation of this technology, there is a real chance that humans will not have to speak anymore as we will communicate by reading each other thoughts completely. Whether this is a good idea or not, we can't know for now, but it could for cure change the course of human evolution in one way or another. With implants in the brain and synthetic replacements of our body, are we already evolving into something or someone who can not be called Homo sapiens anymore? Who knows, perhaps in

100 000 years, historians will mark 2020 as the first evolutionary evidence of new species called Homo Techiens. But constant technological advancements could also take us into disasters that we cannot even think of.

Seventy years ago, no one predicted the internet and what we will create with it. All futuristic movies, books, and articles delved into something completely different during history, such as flying cars, robots et cetera. Not that we don't have those in some kind of experimental phases, but they are not so important currently as the Internet is. The Internet changed every possible thing we can imagine on this planet, some for better, some for worse. So, it is hard to predict what will be the most important technological advancement in the next 1000 years. I mean, as mentioned, no one even predicted the Internet, not even close (ok, to be fair, Marshall McLuhan described something similar in 1962 but not really in a way it is used today), and it has by far the biggest influence on humanity today. Especially having in mind how fast everything is evolving, particularly in the last 20 or 30 years. This rather fast advancement can be described quite nicely with Moore's law. Moore's law simply describes that the number of transistors on integrated circuits doubles on average every two years.

This is rather important since the power of computers is thus increasing almost exponentially. The doubling time of computational power and capacity for PCs was 1,5 between the years 1975 and 2009. Just remember the ENIAC computer, which was the size of an apartment, while today you have much more power in your pocket. It is astonishing yet kind of horrifying. Nevertheless, not all progress is linear as it is with computers. That is to say, we do not see progress every year, but in contrast, one sudden patent can shrink 100 years of development into one year. This non-linearity can be perhaps described with recent findings in the human genome. Let's mention CRISPR here (clustered regularly interspaced short palindromic repeats). CRISPR is a rather simple technology as it seems, but it is a fantastically powerful tool for editing genomes. Just imagine what you could do with such a tool if it is widespread and available for every human. It is technologically available already, but still, there are many concerns. For one, you could edit the genomes of your babies so that they do not get cancer, and this is great. But perhaps rich people could also edit genomes so that their children are way smarter and stronger than other children. Well, Huston, then we have a problem. And a big one.

Nevertheless, with all those linear or non-linear advancements, we will almost inevitably "evolve" into a different kind of human being. Will this be a better or worse version of us, time will tell. But such a progression could also potentially lead to the destruction or extinction of human beings. Luckily invention of nuclear weapons didn't lead to worldwide catastrophic events which would wipe out whole humanity and every living creature, for that matter. Yet. That, however, does not mean that we will not invent something that will destroy us. There are many proponents of Artificial Intelligence (AI), but many opponents also raise concerns about potentially too much power of AI. Nevertheless, there's one thing that many scientists agree with, and this is that perhaps the most probable "development" in the distant future is human extinction. Whether this happens because of some external event such as a big asteroid hitting the Earth or an internal event such as humans destroying our own habitat, we don't know, but the probability is high for this kind of scenario, especially if we extrapolate our thoughts into 100 000 years or millions of years from now.

As best we can tell, and it is a very rough estimate, given the limitations of both our knowledge and our evidence (the latter of which, extensive as it has become in the last century and a half since Darwin, is still grossly small) the average span of any particular species (and the definition of such is a subject of much disagreement) is between 3 and 5 million years old. Exceptionally long-lived species may go 10 million years (and of all the orders and families in taxonomy - turtles/tortoises of the vertebrates have been the most successful in terms of general longevity of their type or closely related types). That may not be a comforting number for humanity because (depending on how we humans are defined) our oldest, arguable antecedent may be as old as 5 million years already. If, however, we count only our emergence as Homo sapiens, then we are only between 200 and 300 thousand years old. So, we do not really know if our group is in its senescence, its "final stage," or freshly sprung and with a grand future before us. And so, one of perhaps most probably next evolutionary steps for Homo sapiens is extinction. But what else do we have? Can we expect some kind of mutations, enlarged or smaller parts of our bodies? The first question that comes to mind while mentioning this topic is – the size of our heads & brains, and are they getting bigger?

Beginning with the dawn of the first Homo species, human heads evolved to be progressively bigger until around 30,000 years ago, when head size plateaued. We actually don't know why size plateaued. But we do know that about 6,000 years ago when agriculture took off, skulls began shrinking. The cause of the shrinkage is also a mystery, but scientists have cautiously agreed that more efficient brain wiring can be tied to easier access to food and safety. This again connects to the idea that people no longer had to be so resourceful and intelligent to survive (Idiocracy rings a bell?).

In either direction, heads or brains getting smaller or getting bigger, we don't have enough data to predict what will happen in 100 000 years with our bodies. We could expect that size of the human body will be somehow smaller or less muscular, and this is because so many people live 100% sedentary life. This trend of not using muscles at all could even increase in the coming years with the explosion of virtual reality, online shopping, and online everything. Sex robots, which are discussed in a separate chapter of this book, could potentially represent the main trigger in shifting paths of human evolution. If most of the population gets addicted to sex robots, this will surely impact our population curve and thus also our evolution in the long run. Could this "phenomenon" also impact the size of sexual organs? We don't know, but it is fun contemplating the idea. Just imagine humans in the year 4023 constantly sitting at home making love with their sex robots, whether those are physically present or virtually but completely realistic and available on demand.

Somehow related or perhaps unrelated, but worth mentioning here is the rise of the transgender community. Let's just indulge the idea that a significant proportion of humans decide to be transgender. How will that impact our population and evolution? Will we become completely asexual and non-fertile in the future? Well, the possibility is there for sure. And so, I digress here on human sexuality, and while it is a rather important part of life, again, we can't be sure how it will evolve (or devolve) in thousand years, but it is fascinating to wonder.

Moving on to a more scientifically backed approach. With recent advancements in DNA techniques, we have some real proof of what has been happening in an evolutionary sense for the last thousands of years. By using those DNA techniques, we found out that perhaps the rate of human evolution is actually increasing. Namely, we underwent the most dramatic changes to our bodies when our species first appeared. Similarly, in modern times it is clear that we as a species are showing genetically induced changes to our physiology. Some clues to confirm that can be seen in the fact that human races around the world are becoming more rather than less distinguished. This obviously contradicts my imaginary hypothesis that perhaps in 10000 years, we will all be (mostly) the same race. Yet again, as we can see, evolution does not follow some linear or even logical path. Everybody would have thought that naturally, our heads and brains would become bigger while the opposite is happening. So, the same analogy can be drawn with races. Even though some DNA techniques today show that human races are becoming more distinct, this could easily change with some invention or big event which will change the course of evolution. As we know, agriculture had a big impact on how humans evolved. Modern technology as a set of inventions is still in its infancy compared to agriculture, and we have no idea how it will impact us in the long run.

We constantly carry our mobile phones with us and look at them as the most important thing. Some day will they become part of us entirely? Some people say that we are already somehow cyborgs because our smartphones are our prolonged artifact for information and communication. The challenge currently is bandwidth limitation between us and our smartphones. That limitation is represented in our hands and eyes. Think of it as a mouse and keyboard that we use to control our computer. Well, the hypothesis is - one day, we'll remove that limitation and achieve a complete merger with computers; thus, I/O (Input / Output) bandwidth would become unbelievable. This could be the final trigger for singularity (if it didn't happen already). Singularity, in this sense, is a theoretical point in time at which technological growth becomes overwhelming and irreversible, resulting in unforeseeable changes to human civilization.

Those unforeseeable and overwhelming changes to us, Homo sapiens, could be, as mentioned before, the complete coalescence of biological bodies and computers. In some way, those things are already happening today with experimental implants, which are now used for basic things such as buying stuff in grocery stores. But advancement in technology and our desire to constantly develop will take it much further. There will be good and wise implementations benefiting the whole society of humans, and there will be greedy, wicked, and weird implementations that could again completely change the course of our evolution. Which one will win will decide what will become of us in hundreds and thousands of years. No one has even the slightest idea, as no one from 500 years predicted anything similar to what is happening today. Humans are (biologically) the same in that span of time, but almost everything else is different. Even the smaller span of time applies. If you're in your 30's just ask your mother or father did they even dream that one day people would willingly upload their pictures to the world so everyone can see them instantly. Or that they would carry some screens with them all the time, having the ability to look at any information possible and watch the weirdest pornography imaginable. Anyone proposing this idea 70 years ago would have been called a crazy maniac. Well, here we are, while biologically the same, 180 degrees different than our grandparents were. In the next hundred and surely thousand years, we will not be even biologically the same. We can call this evolution, progression, or perhaps digression. Contrasted to previous times, we'll have all videos and pictures as proof for comparison. This wasn't the case in any previous millennia. Of course, if some big disaster doesn't hit the Earth as it did many, many times in history. Interesting times ahead for humanity, or should I say for beyond humanity.

Research is formalized curiosity. it is poking and prying with a purpose.

—ZORA NEALE HURSTON

BIBLIOGRAPHY

Bagdikian, B. H. (2004). *The New Media Monopoly: A Completely Revised and Updated Edition With Seven New Chapters*. Beacon Press; 20th ed. edition.

Barthes, R. (2013). *Mythologies*. Hill & Wang.

Becker, E. (2010). *Birth and Death of Meaning*. Free Press.

Bezzerides, A. (2021). *Evolution Gone Wrong: The Curious Reasons Why Our Bodies Work (Or Don't)*. HarperCollins Publishers.

Black, M. C., Basile, K. C., Breiding, M. J., & Smith, S. G. (2010). *The National Intimate Partner and Sexual Violence Survey: 2010 Summary Report*. CDC, Division of Violence Prevention. Retrieved from https://www.cdc.gov/violenceprevention/pdf/nisvs_executive_summary-a.pdf

Bok, S. (2011). *Lying: Moral Choice in Public and*

Private Life. Vintage.

Bolhuis, J. J., & Hogan, J. A. (1999). *The Development of Animal Behavior: A Reader 1st Edition.* Wiley-Blackwell.

Borders, M. (2018). *The Social Singularity: How decentralization will allow us to transcend politics, create global prosperity, and avoid the robot apocalypse.* Social Evolution.

Bradshaw, S., Bailey, H., & Howard, P. N. (2020). Industrialized Disinformation: 2020 Global Inventory of Organized Social Media Manipulation. *Computational Propaganda Research Project (University of Oxford).*

Bush, R. A. (2021). *Designing the Mind: The Principles of Psychitecture.* Designing the Mind: The Principles of Psychitecture.

Campbell, R. N. (1981). *Royal Investigations of the Origin of Language.* Retrieved from https://www.researchgate.net/publication/233 597995_Royal_Investigations_of_the_Origin_of_L anguage

Cimino, A. (n.d.). *The Manhattan Project.*

Coyne, J. A. (2009). *Why Evolution Is True.* Penguin Books.

Coyne, J. A. (2015). *Faith Versus Fact: Why Science and Religion Are Incompatible.* Penguin Books.

Danaher, J. (2017). *Robot Sex: Social and Ethical Implications.* The MIT Press.

Darwin, C. (2009). *The Origin Of Species: 150th*

Anniversary Edition. Signet; Reprint, Anniversary edition.

Dice, M. (2020). *Hollywood Propaganda: How TV, Movies, and Music Shape Our Culture*. The Resistance Manifesto.

Feldman, R. S. (2002). Retrieved from University of Massachusetts: https://www.umass.edu/newsoffice/article/umass-amherst-researcher-finds-most-people-lie-everyday-conversation

Firstenberg, A. (2020). *The Invisible Rainbow: A History of Electricity and Life*. Chelsea Green Publishing.

Ford, I. (2020, September 22). *top-10-weirdest-laws-around-world*. Retrieved from TheLawyerPortal: https://www.thelawyerportal.com/blog/top-10-weirdest-laws-around-world/

Gorvett, Z. (2020). *How the news changes the way we think and behave* . Retrieved from BBC: https://www.bbc.com/future/article/20200512-how-the-news-changes-the-way-we-think-and-behave

Grant, A. (2021). *Think Again: The Power of Knowing What You Don't Know*. Viking.

Harari, Y. N. (2014). *Sapiens: A Brief History of Humankind*. Vintage Digital; 1st edition .

HARNESS, J. (2012, May). *The 9 Worst Moms in the Animal Kingdom*. Retrieved from Mental Floss: https://www.mentalfloss.com/article/30657/9-

worst-moms-animal-kingdom

Harris, S. (2012). *Free Will*. Free Press.

Harris, S., & Harris, A. (2013). *Lying* . Four Elephants
Press.

Heinlein, R. A. (1988). *Time Enough for Love*. Ace;
Reissue edition.

Hemp, P. (2009, September). *Harward Business
Review*. Retrieved from Death by Information
Overload: https://hbr.org/2009/09/death-by-
information-overload

Holiday, R. (2019). *Trust Me, I'm Lying: Confessions of a
Media Manipulator*.

Huff, M., & Higdon, N. (2019). *United States of
Distraction: Media Manipulation in Post-Truth
America (And What We Can Do About It)*. City
Lights Publishers.

Jagan, V. a. (2016). "Early Intervention and Diagnosis
of Autism.". *Indian Journal of Health and
Wellbeing, vol. 7, no. 12, Indian Association of
Health, Research and Welfare, p. 1144*.

Kaufman, S. B. (2020). *Transcend: The New Science of
Self-Actualization*. TarcherPerigee.

Kennett, D. (2012). *The Surnames Handbook: A Guide
to Family Name Research in the 21st Century*.
The History Press.

Lanier, J. (2013). *Who Owns the Future?* Simon &
Schuster.

Lanier, J. (2018). *Ten Arguments for Deleting Your
Social Media Accounts Right Now*. Henry Holt

and Co.

Levy, D. (2008). *Love and Sex with Robots: The Evolution of Human-Robot Relationships.* Harper Perennial .

Lewis, W. (2014). *What's in Your Surname?: The Fascinating Story of British Surnames (History of English Names Book 1).* Brazen Head Publishing.

Lissa Poirot. (2020). *Far&Wide.* Retrieved from weird-laws-world: https://www.farandwide.com/s/weird-laws-world-4961c1ede8d749bf

Maslow, A. H. (2015). *Toward a Psychology of Being.* Sublime Books.

McIntosh, M. A. (2020, October 1). *A Brief History of Law since the Ancient World.* Retrieved from Brewminate: https://brewminate.com/a-brief-history-of-law-since-the-ancient-world/

Milham, S. (2012). *Dirty Electricity: Electrification and the Diseases of Civilization.* iUniverse .

Minger, D. (2014). *Death by Food Pyramid: How Shoddy Science, Sketchy Politics and Shady Special Interests Have Ruined Our Health.* Primal Nutrition, Inc.

Musman, R. (1987). *Background to English-speaking Countries.* Macmillan Education; 1st edition.

Northrup, D. (2013). *How English Became the Global Language.* Palgrave Macmillan; 2013th edition (March 20, 2013).

Oates, J. (2012). *Tracing Your Ancestors from 1066 to*

1837: A Guide for Family Historians. Pen &
Sword.

Our world in data. (2019). Retrieved from Life
Expetancy: https://ourworldindata.org/life-
expectancy

Parker, C. A. (2015). *Master of Electricity - Nikola Tesla:
A Quick-Read Biography About the Life and
Inventions of a Visionary Genius (Volume 5)*.
CreateSpace Independent Publishing Platform.

Price, N. J. (2017). *The Encyclopedia of American Last
Names: Family Genealogy and Meanings for
1000 Surnames of Early European Settlers to the
United States*. Synchronista LLC.

Rhodes, R. (2009). *Manhattan Project: The Birth of the
Atomic Bomb in the Words of Its Creators,
Eyewitnesses, and Historians*. Black Dog &
Leventhal.

Richman, S. (1994). *Separating School & State: How to
Liberate America's Families*.

Sahija, L. (2018, January). *Scientists Spot the Earliest
Roots of Empathy in How Babies Process Touch*.
Retrieved from TheSwaddle:
https://theswaddle.com/baby-brain-activity-
shows-how-infants-learn-empathy-through-
tough/

Sartore, R. L. (1991). The Link between Mythology and
Education. *The Clearing House: A Journal of
Educational Strategies, Issues and Ideas R*.

Scarborough, P., Appleby, P. N., Mizdrak, A., Briggs, A.

D., Travis, R. C., Bradbury, K. E., & Key, T. J. (2014). *NCBI*. Retrieved from Dietary greenhouse gas emissions of meat-eaters, fish-eaters, vegetarians and vegans in the UK: https://www.ncbi.nlm.nih.gov/pmc/articles/PMC4372775/

ScienceDaily. (2019, March 15). Retrieved from ScienceDaily: https://www.sciencedaily.com/releases/2019/03/190315110908.htm

Shattuck, R. (1994). *The Forbidden Experiment: The Story of the Wild Boy of Aveyron (Kodansha Globe)*. Kodansha Globe; Reprint edition (October 15, 1994).

Shaw, G. B. (n.d.). *Pygmalion*. 2018: CreateSpace Independent Publishing Platform.

Shubin, N. (2020). *Some Assembly Required: Decoding Four Billion Years of Life, from Ancient Fossils to DNA*. neworld Publications.

Singer, P. W. (2018). *LikeWar: The Weaponization of Social Media*. Mariner Books; Reprint edition.

Stafford, T. (2014, August 4). *Why bad news dominates the headlines* . Retrieved from Mindhacks: https://mindhacks.com/2014/08/04/why-bad-news-dominates-the-headlines/

STPauls. (n.d.). Retrieved from US Experiment on infants withholding affectio: https://stpauls.vxcommunity.com/Issue/Us-Experiment-On-Infants-Withholding-

Affection/13213

Szabo, A., & Hopkinson, K. L. (2007). *Pubmed*.
Retrieved from NCBI:
https://pubmed.ncbi.nlm.nih.gov/17926432/

Tesla, N. (2018). *My Inventions: The Autobiography of Nikola Tesla*. GENERAL PRESS.

Tomassi, R. (2013). *The Rational Male*.

Vine, D. (2020). *The United States of War: A Global History of America's Endless Conflicts, from Columbus to the Islamic State*. University of California Press.

Waal, F. d. (2007). *Chimpanzee Politics: Power and Sex among Apes*. Johns Hopkins University Press.

Watts, A. W. (2012). *Wisdom Of Insecurity: A Message for an Age of Anxiety*. Ebury Digital.

Watts, A. W. (2018). *The Meaning of Happiness: The Quest for Freedom of the Spirit in Modern Psychology and the Wisdom of the East*. New World Library.

Watts, A. W. (2021). *The Way of Zen*. Ebury Digital.

WHO. (2021). Retrieved from Diabetes - WHO: https://www.who.int/news-room/fact-sheets/detail/diabetes

About the Author

Born and raised in Croatia, Domagoj Pernar was always a curious fellow. From his young days, he was interested in many different topics ranging from Russian authors such as Dostoevsky to interests in computers, informatics science, and mechanics. Later in life, he started researching philosophical theories and the potential for a dystopian end of society (perhaps that's why he was born in 1984.) These interests in the philosophy and meaning of life, potential future developments of the world, and overall curiosity about today's (and past) world led to the creation of this book. The book that can be classified as semi-fiction and semi non-fiction. For more info about potential future projects or if you wish to contact the author, please reach out directly on CuriousMatrix.com

The important thing is not to stop questioning. Curiosity has its own reason for existing. One cannot help but be in awe when he contemplates the mysteries of eternity, of life, of the marvelous structure of reality. It is enough if one tries merely to comprehend a little of this mystery every day.

— ALBERT EINSTEIN

Made in the USA
Coppell, TX
30 December 2021

70371867R00118